Doris Stokes is a celebrated clairaudient who has
confounded sceptics by the uncanny accuracy of her
readings. In Australia she filled the Sydney Opera House
and was mobbed in the streets. In America, 'Charlie's
Angels' was removed from a prime television slot to make
way for her. In this country her appearances on radio
phone-ins have caused an avalanche of mail. In her first
book, VOICES IN MY EAR, Doris told how she
discovered in herself this extraordinary gift and how she
has shared it with the world. In MORE VOICES IN MY
EAR she continued her story and now INNOCENT
VOICES IN MY EAR tells the stories of her 'spirit
children'.

Also by Doris Stokes

VOICES IN MY EAR: THE AUTOBIOGRAPHY OF A MEDIUM
MORE VOICES IN MY EAR
A HOST OF VOICES
WHISPERING VOICES
VOICES OF LOVE

Doris Stokes
with Linda Dearsley

# Innocent Voices
# In My Ear

Futura

A Futura Book

First published in Great Britain in 1983
by Futura Publications, a Division of
Macdonald & Co (Publishers) Ltd
Reprinted 1983, 1984 (twice), 1985 (three times), 1987

ISBN 0 7088 2320 3

Filmset, printed and bound in Great Britain by
Hazell Watson & Viney Limited,
Member of the BPCC Group,
Aylesbury, Bucks

Futura Publications
A Division of
Macdonald & Co (Publishers) Ltd
Greater London House
Hampstead Road
London NW1 7QX
A BPCC plc Company

# AUTHOR'S NOTE

Doris Stokes would like to apologize to the parents of all those children who are not mentioned in this book. Vital tapes containing the details of many case histories were stolen in transit, and she has been unable to recall them all. She can only hope that the person responsible will feel thoroughly ashamed when he or she listens to the heartbreak and tragedy recorded.

I dedicate this book to one of
nature's gentlemen, Dick Emery,
who loved children as much as I do.

I would like to thank all those who have
so kindly provided me with photographs
of their children – and only wish that
all could have been printed in this book.

'Death is nothing at all. I have only slipped
away into the next room. I am I and you are you.
Whatever we were to each other, that we are still.

Call me by my old familiar name; speak to me
in the easy way which you always used; put no
difference in your tone; wear no forced air of
solemnity or sorrow; laugh, as we always laughed
at the little jokes we enjoyed together; pray,
smile, think of me, pray for me; let my name be
ever the household word that it always was;
let it be spoken without effect, without the trace
of a shadow on it.

Life means all that it ever meant; it is the same
as it ever was; there is unbroken continuity.
Why should I be out of mind because I am out of
sight? I am waiting for you, for an interval,
somewhere very near – Just around the corner.
All is well.'

*With thanks to Mandy's mother, Jill,
for the comfort her words have given to
parents over the world*

# CHAPTER 1

The boy appeared almost immediately. He was a small, neat child, maybe four or five years old, with dark brown hair that waved softly round his head and a pointed little face like that of an elf.

He grinned at me and I smiled back, but then my attention was diverted by something his relatives were saying. Moments later a flash of movement caught my eye. I glanced round and there he was – stripping off his clothes. Off came his jumper, off came his jeans, off came his socks, off came his underwear, and as he finished with each garment he flung it to the floor. Finally, when he was naked as the day he was born, he stood in front of me, pink, dimpled and pleased with himself.

I started to laugh.

'What's the joke?' asked the boy's father because, not being a medium, he couldn't see what had happened.

'The cheeky young beggar!' I chuckled. 'He's just taken off all his clothes and thrown them on the floor. He's standing there in the nudie!'

But, to my surprise, the man didn't laugh. He started to cry. 'That's the only evidence I need,' he said. 'Paul was mentally retarded and we used to apologize to guests in advance because if he thought he was being ignored he used to take his clothes off.'

Little Paul had died or, as I would say, passed on some months before, but, although his family could no longer see him, he wasn't very far away. He hadn't changed. He wasn't mentally handicapped any more, of course, but his personality was still the same. He thought he was being ignored when I talked to someone else, so off came his clothes!

I've always been daft about children and I think that's why, even today, my communications with the other side are particularly vivid if there's a child involved. Even as a child myself I loved the little ones smaller than me and I genuinely thought all babies were beautiful. From the earliest age I would beg to cuddle them and change their nappies. Dolls didn't interest me if there was a real live baby around.

'Pol,' young mothers used to say (for some reason everyone called me Polly in those days), 'come and hold our so and so's bottle.'

And I'd stand there beside the pram, barely tall enough to see over the side, proudly holding the bottle until the baby had finished. Then, standing on tiptoe, I carefully wiped its face and mouth.

Even in those days I was getting a helping hand from the spirit world, although I was too young to realize it then. I remember the day I met a neighbour trundling her heavy old pram along the streets of Grantham where I was born. The sight of that pram was like a magnet to me and I was at her side in seconds. The baby was sitting there in his frilly sun bonnet, tiny fists waving, and I'll swear he smiled when he saw me. I skipped along with the pram for a while, shaking his rattle and pulling funny faces to make him laugh, but in the end I could contain myself no longer.

'Oh, can I have a push?' I burst out, and the woman laughed.

'Go on then, Pol,' she said, probably glad of a rest, 'but just mind what you're doing, that's all.'

She moved aside and I took her place on the handle. Proudly, and with infinite care, I manoeuvred the pram over every crack and bump and soon I was bowling along as if to the manner born. It was all going well – I'd even managed the kerbstone smoothly – when suddenly the baby began to cough.

At first his mother smiled and patted him indulgently on the back, but as the coughing grew worse and he turned scarlet in the face, she became seriously alarmed.

'Whatever's the matter?' she cried, unstrapping him and shooting me an accusing glance as if she suspected it was my fault.

Frightened, I stared at the sobbing child. I was only pushing the pram but could I have done something wrong? What's the matter with him, I wondered guiltily. Instantly, as if a voice had spoken in my head, came the answer. He's got a peanut stuck in his throat.

'He's got a peanut stuck in his throat,' I blurted aloud, without pausing to question how I knew.

The woman stared at me, then put her finger into the baby's mouth. A split second later out came an unchewed nut. Apparently she had been eating peanuts a little while before and, thinking the baby was old enough to cope with them, she'd given him a couple. He must have kept one unchewed in his cheek and forgotten about it until it went down the wrong way.

At any rate, my answer had been right.

'But, Pol,' said our neighbour as she settled the baby back in his place, 'how did . . . ?' Then she stopped, her expression uneasy. 'Yes, well I think I'd better carry on pushing now,' she finished briskly and sadly I was forced to relinquish the pram.

Throughout my childhood I came to know that expression very well. I would say something quite innocent, intending to be helpful, and an adult face would change from relief to suspicion and then wariness. You could almost hear them thinking, 'But how does she know these things?' Had I not been an ordinary, down-to-earth child,

13

good old Sam and Jenny Sutton's little girl, I think they might have been frightened of me. As it was, they were uneasy but I did have some reassuring saving graces. I was a proper little mother and that they approved of, although my involvement with the little ones didn't always do me any good.

When I was a little older I used to take out baby Hazel Hudson, the youngest of our neighbours' children. I went for long walks with the pram, chattering away to Hazel who couldn't understand a word but who gurgled obligingly as if we were having a proper conversation. So when Hazel's brother and sister, Kenny and Joyce, caught scarlet fever and were sent to the isolation hospital it was only natural that Mrs Hudson should ask me to take Hazel to visit them when she wasn't able to go herself.

I didn't mind a bit. The hospital was outside the town, and it was a pleasant walk. As it happened it was a lovely day in the early spring with the tips of crocus just showing above the ground. It was so nice, in fact, that my sister Edna and her friend Peggy decided to come with me.

It was an enjoyable outing. Hazel was well behaved as usual and the rest of us were in high spirits. We knocked on the door of the hospital to hand in the sweets and comics Mrs Hudson had packed up, then we walked round to the window of the children's ward. We weren't allowed inside, of course, but we waved and shouted to Joyce and Kenny through the glass, and I think we cheered them up.

That should have been the end of my good deed. But the following week I began to feel unwell. My head ached, my temperature soared and, by the weekend, I was being raced back to the isolation hospital by ambulance. As they carried me up the path on a stretcher I pushed the blankets off my face.

'Don't do that, love,' said the ambulance man, pushing them back again.

'I only wanted to see if the crocuses were out,' I muttered.

But it was too late. We were through the door and heading for the children's ward where I'd be able to cheer Joyce and Kenny from the inside this time. Of the four of us who'd set out that spring afternoon to visit the Hudson children, I was the only one who caught scarlet fever.

I suppose I picked up quite a few childhood illnesses that way but it didn't deter me. As I grew up I was always surrounded by children and when I eventually married it came as no surprise to anyone that I wanted a baby right away.

Well, I got my wish. I had my baby and that baby was to change my life for ever. As I explained in my first book, *Voices in My Ear*, my little John Michael was taken from me when he was just five months old. Blockage of the bowel, they said. They operated on him but it was no use. He died soon afterwards.

It was the tragedy of my life. When you lose a mother or a father or even a much-loved husband it's bad enough, but when you lose a child it's the worst thing that can happen. That child is part of you and when the child dies part of you dies with him.

Sadly, I was unable to have any more children though I was lucky enough to adopt a little boy called Terry who is with us still. Yet, out of that tragedy something wonderful happened. Inconsolable with grief I drifted from church to church until I ended up at a spiritualist meeting. There, at last, I got proof from the medium that my son was not really dead, that he was happy and well and being looked after by his grandad on 'the other side'.

Naturally, I wanted to know more. My mother had always been very much against 'they spiritualists' and continually warned me about them. I'd end up in a mental home if I had anything to do with them, she reckoned. But they were the only ones who'd been able to offer me any comfort and I was determined to find out what their organization was about.

That's how it all began. Gradually, I realized that I was a natural medium. Hundreds of strange little incidents over the years fell into place and I began to develop my powers. If I hadn't lost John Michael my gift might have remained unused and undeveloped. Though I would gladly have traded all my powers just to hold my baby in my arms again it was nice to think that his life hadn't been in vain. Through John Michael I was able to help hundreds, and eventually thousands, of people all over the world.

Today I work on all sorts of cases, from haunted houses and unsolved murders to public meetings in vast stadiums and private sittings for bereaved relatives. Yet I've noticed that, without exception, over the years my most successful sittings have been with mothers who've lost children.

I am convinced this is because of John Michael. Unless you've lost a child yourself you can't truly understand the complex emotions that tear you apart.

When I got back from the hospital that terrible day the first thing I said was: 'What have I done to deserve this? I must have been very bad somewhere.' You feel you're being punished. You feel guilty. You think, Was it my fault? Was there something else I could have done?

No matter how the child died and no matter how illogical it sounds, you blame yourself.

Of course, everyone tells you that time is a great healer but the months wear on and the guilt gives way to desolation and the grief lies like a block of ice right across your solar plexus. If you smoke, you smoke too much; if you drink, you drink too much; nothing does any good. Every morning I woke up thinking it was all a nightmare, that I'd glance across and see my baby playing happily in his cot waiting for me to rise. Then I'd remember and it would hit me all over again. There was no baby, the cot was cold and empty, and the nightmare was real.

At the time it all seemed so senseless and there were days when I wanted to die. But now, years later, I know that it did make sense, there was a purpose to my suffering. Now, when a sitter walks through my door, I can tell immediately if she's lost a child and that common experience strengthens the psychic power. Often I see the child before the mother's even got her coat off.

This sense of affinity was particularly strong when I met recently a young woman called Denise. I knew she'd lost a child, but there was something more than that and it puzzled me. The feeling nagged as I went into the kitchen to put the kettle on for our usual cup of tea before the sitting. When I went back into the living-room I had the sensation of a baby being put into my arms and I realized what that something was. Denise, like me, had lost a baby boy, at five months old. What's more, being particularly sensitive, she'd had a premonition about his death weeks before, just as I did about John Michael.

Denise was divorced and looked after her new husband's three children as well as her daughter from her first marriage, but, apart from that difference in our lives, I could have been meeting myself thirty years before.

After the sitting Denise explained what happened before her baby died. Like me she hardly dared talk about her fears in case people thought she was mad.

'My first husband died unexpectedly just a few weeks before Nathan was born,' she said. 'It hit me pretty hard because, although we were divorced, I was still fond of him. Anyway, Nathan was born and I forgot about the shock because there was a lot of worry over him. He was a perfect little boy but he was premature and only weighed three pounds.

'It was a difficult start for him but he seemed to do well. I brought him home and he was settling down and the children were fascinated by him. Then one day a few weeks later I was sitting by the fire when from nowhere the thought suddenly came into my head: "Len had to go so that he could look after Nathan". I hadn't even been thinking about my ex-husband. It sounds crazy but instantly I just knew that this idea was right. I was so certain, I burst into tears, ran in a panic to check Nathan and then when I was sure he was all right I phoned my sister.

' "Nathan's going to die!" I sobbed.'

Denise's sister obviously thought Denise was suffering from the strain and worry of the premature birth. She made soothing noises, pointed out how healthy Nathan had become and told her to calm down.

'I felt I'd been silly,' said Denise, 'but I couldn't get the idea out of my mind. Yet the weeks went by and Nathan was fine. In the end I thought I must have been imagining things.'

Like John Michael, Nathan was an exceptionally good baby. He never cried. He was always happy. He'd let anyone pick him up. He seemed to need an unusual amount of sleep and he rarely woke of his own accord. Most mornings Denise had to wake him for his feed, but when she mentioned this to anyone else they just said she should think herself lucky. With four other children to care for as well, she soon forgot the strange premonition. Or at least her conscious mind forgot.

'Over the next few months I kept having this weird dream,' said Denise. 'Usually I dream in colour but this dream was in black and white, like an old photograph. There was a group of people standing around chatting and laughing as if they were having a lovely time. But as I looked at them I realized they were all dead. They were people I'd known in the past who'd later died. But as I watched I had this strong feeling of being pulled up -- as if they were pulling me up to them to join the party. I shouted out, "I can't come." Then I'd wake up.

'About this time I was looking through a shopping catalogue and I decided to buy a black suit. Now, black is a colour I never wear. I look really dreadful in black and for that reason I haven't got any black clothes. Yet, although I couldn't say why, I was convinced I should spend quite a lot of money on this suit which probably would look horrible. My sister couldn't understand it. "What on earth d'you want that for?" she asked. And I don't know what made me say it but I replied, "Oh, it'll come in handy for the odd funeral." '

Three months later Denise was driving home from a shopping trip in Shrewsbury when she suddenly became alarmed and stopped the car.

'I felt very strange,' she said. 'The pulling up feeling I'd had in my dream was back and very strong and there was death all around. I know it sounds crazy. Hysterical if you like. I can't explain it but, without doubt, death was very close. I looked over at Nathan but he was sleeping peacefully and I thought it was me who was going to die. It had been snowing and everything was very white and unnaturally sharp as if I was looking through binoculars, and all the time I was being pulled up.

'Death was so close I actually cried out loud, "Oh no, not me. I've got all the children to look after." I don't know whether that helped but gradually the feeling drained away and everything was normal again. I sat there a bit longer feeling shaky and wondering what had happened. Then I remembered the children would be coming home from school so I went back.

'Nathan seemed fine. There was nothing wrong with him at all. It was me I felt the warning was for. That night I put him in his cot as usual and he was quite happy. The next morning I went to get him up and he was dead.'

The doctors told Denise that her baby was a cot death victim. Very little is known about cot death beyond the fact that it is a silent killer which strikes apparently healthy babies without warning. It is more common in premature babies like Nathan than full-term children, they said, and they thought the fact that Nathan slept so much was probably significant, but that was all they could tell her.

It wasn't much comfort and, as the months went by, Denise didn't seem to get any better. She didn't care what happened to her, life didn't seem worth living, and she vaguely realized that she wasn't being fair to the rest of the family. In desperation she wrote to me.

At the time of the sitting, of course, I knew nothing about the whole sad story apart from the fact she'd lost a child. Then as I walked back into the sitting-room and I felt the baby in my arms I looked down and saw that it was a beautiful little fellow, with fairish hair curling into ringlets all over his head. He looked between five and a half and six months old and he was chuckling away. As I admired him a voice told me that Denise had one other child of her own and three of her second husband's children and that this baby, who was their first joint child, had gone to sleep and woken up on the other side.

Denise confirmed that this was right. Then a strong male voice with a Welsh accent interrupted. He said he was Denise's husband and he'd gone over very quickly with a heart attack.

'I still love her,' he told me, 'and for the love we had I have taken her son and made him mine. We couldn't live together but I still love her.' I thought he said his name was Ken but I misheard.

'Len,' Denise corrected.

Len kept going back over the failed marriage. It obviously worried him that he hadn't been able to make Denise understand how he felt for her when they lived together and he wanted to put it right now.

'It wasn't my wish to split up,' he insisted. 'I would have laid down my life for her but I couldn't communicate with her in the end. She always seemed beyond my reach. I thought, whatever she wants I'll agree to, but perhaps I was wrong. Maybe I should have worked harder at it. I shouldn't have let her go.'

He was also worried about the other children. Like many mothers in the same position Denise had sent all her love away with Nathan. She fed and cared for the other children in practical ways but emotionally she'd shut them out.

'Tell her to go home and give Emma Louise a big cuddle and the other three as well,' Len asked. But when I passed the message to Denise she began to cry.

'I can't, I can't,' she sobbed. 'All my love has gone with Nathan.'

This often happens and it's very sad for the children who're left because they don't understand what's happened. Their little brother or sister has mysteriously gone away and won't come back and mummy snaps at them and doesn't smile any more. You don't know what goes through little children's minds. Often they think they must be to blame. Their parents seem to be angry with them so they think the death must somehow be their fault.

'Denise, you must try,' I begged her. 'It's not fair on the other children. You must give them more attention,

21

particularly Emma Louise. She adored her little brother and she misses him terribly.'

Denise dried her eyes and promised that she would try, although she didn't know whether she would be success-ful.

The sitting went on and her mother, Hetty, came back to talk to her and mentioned the name Lilian.

'That's my real name,' Denise admitted with a smile, 'but I never liked it and everyone calls me Denise.'

As she spoke, a light almost like a torch beam suddenly appeared and started dancing about near her shoulder. I realized that someone else had joined us with a message. It was a man. He'd been over three years, he said, he'd passed with cancer and he belonged to Margaret.

'Margaret's a friend,' said Denise slowly. 'Oh, that must be her husband, Bill. He died three years ago of cancer.' She was puzzled, however, as to why Bill should turn up during the sitting because she hadn't known him very well during his lifetime. Why had he bothered to come? It was only afterwards when she met Margaret that it fell into place.

'Margaret said she wasn't a bit surprised,' Denise wrote to me later, 'because, although I didn't realize it at the time, the day of the sitting was the anniversary of the day he died.'

That special day Bill was obviously thinking of Mar-garet and when he spotted the communication lines open with one of her friends he didn't want to miss the chance of letting her know he was all right and he hadn't forgotten.

You often hear people say that grief brings couples together but sadly I've found this isn't always true. Sometimes parents become marooned in their sorrow, isolated from each other and unable to show their feelings.

The longer it goes on the higher the barrier between them grows and the more difficult it becomes to break it down.

I was reminded of this soon after Denise's visit when another young mother came to see me. Her name was Theresa and she was a pretty girl with dark curly hair and a look of hope in her eyes. It was only as the sitting progressed that I discovered the real tragedy her looks belied. It was nine years since she'd lost her son and in all those years she and her husband had never spoken of him, nor looked at his photograph. It was as if that child had never existed. Now, that's what I call a tragedy.

The sitting started in a light-hearted way. Two young voices came bubbling through. By the sound of them it was a boy and either a girl or a younger boy with a light childish voice. They were giggling and chattering to each other as well as to me, and they were messing about so much it was difficult to make out what they were saying.

'I've got two voices here,' I explained to Theresa. 'Did two children pass over?'

'Yes, but not both mine,' she said. 'One was my sister's.'

It turned out that they were both boys and, after sending their love to various members of the family, I asked them what had happened. There was much excited interrupting of each other but finally we got it straight. One had been ill and the other had had an accident.

As we talked, a sharp pain exploded across the back of my neck.

'I'm not sure which one it is, Theresa,' I said, 'but the back of my neck hurts.'

'That's my son,' she said quickly.

'Well, he was the one who was killed,' I said as the pain subsided. I asked him for his last impressions. 'I'm falling,' he said, 'and then there's a pain in my neck and nothing else.'

'Yes, that's right,' whispered Theresa. 'He fell from some scaffolding and broke his neck.'

As she spoke I had a fleeting impression of a vivid young face suddenly pressed against hers and her son's arms went round her neck in a quick hug. Theresa was very dark but her son was fair, almost blond, with bright unusually blue eyes. His name was Gary. It was nine years since he'd passed and he wanted to give his love to his father, Tony, and his brother Kevin.

'Mummy could look at me, you know, after it happened,' he explained, going back to the accident, 'because my face wasn't even marked.'

His father seemed to be particularly on his mind. 'I'm very proud of my dad,' he said, 'but he finds it hard to talk about me.'

Theresa agreed this was true, but Gary kept returning to it. 'My mum and dad didn't talk to each other for a long time.'

I hesitated. 'Should you be telling me this, Gary?' I asked.

He seemed to think he should.

'Well, what does he mean, Theresa?' I asked. 'Does he mean you didn't talk about him to each other?'

'Yes,' said Theresa. 'We still don't.'

The whole story came out. Since Gary's accident they hadn't mentioned his name, spoken of him, looked at his picture or displayed a photograph in the house. A stranger would never know they'd ever had another son apart from Kevin. It was one of the saddest things I'd ever heard. I didn't know whether to feel more sorry for Gary or for Theresa and her husband.

'Look, love, you're hurting Gary,' I explained gently. 'He's still your son. He still comes to your home and he thinks of himself as one of the family. But you're shutting him out. When small children go over they are brought

24

back by their relatives to visit their parents and they are hurt if it seems the parents don't want to know them any more. You can't just close the door and think if we don't talk about him it'll be as if it never happened. It doesn't work like that. You've borne your grief individually, you've never had a good cry on each other's shoulders, but it would help you so much if you could share it.'

'But it hurts to talk about him,' Theresa sobbed.

'Yes, but you're hurting Gary too, and I know you wouldn't have him hurt for the world. Get his picture out, no matter what Tony says. It will help. My son John Michael will be thirty-eight years old this year but every night before I go to bed I say "Goodnight, God bless you," and first thing in the morning when I come out of the bedroom I go to his picture and say "Morning, my love. How's all the crowd?" I miss him still, of course I do, and there are times when I say "If only . . ." but I can enjoy my life because I know he's all right and I'll see him again one day.'

I wasn't just saying this to cheer Theresa. It is quite true. To this day whenever I feel down and I get into one of my "If only . . ." moods, a great sense of peace and love will suddenly flood over me and I know that, although I can't see him, John Michael has come to reassure me that he's there.

I wasn't sure how much of this advice Theresa could take in in one go but I felt it was very important to try. I couldn't bear the thought of poor Gary going backwards and forwards for nine years to see his parents, only to find they'd shut him out.

I'm glad to say it obviously struck Theresa in the same light. Soon after the sitting I received a letter from her.

'When I got home from seeing you,' she wrote, 'for the first time in nine years, Tony and I were able to sit down and talk about Gary and get out his photographs . . .'

25

So, if I do nothing else this year, I know I've done something worthwhile . . .

I remember so well, the day I had proof that John Michael still lived, a load was lifted off my back.

If I had had £10,000 to give the medium who told me, it would not have been enough. There just is not enough money in the world to pay for that wonderful joy and truth. It's given through God's love so it is beyond price.

# CHAPTER 2

I was standing in a house I'd never seen before. There was a bright, well-furnished living-room with a bay window at one end and a view of the garden at the other, but it was the fireplace that drew my attention.

On the wall beside the chimney breast was a large picture of a striking young girl with shoulder-length brown hair and wide expressive eyes with the hint of a smile in their depths. It was those eyes that held me. There was something oddly compelling about them. It was only a picture yet, no matter where you went in the room, when you glanced up those eyes seemed to be looking straight at you. You had the strangest feeling that when you turned your back, the expression on the girl's face changed and that if only you could spin round quickly enough, you'd catch it before it froze into its painted smile once more.

'It's me, isn't it, Doris? D'you like it?' said a voice beside my ear and I realized that Gail Kinchin was proudly showing me the portrait that now hung in her parents' living-room. The portrait that had been painted after her tragic death.

I gazed at it a moment longer, then the scene shifted and crumbled before my eyes, and I was back in my own flat with Gail's mother Josie sitting opposite me. But Gail was still there.

'It's true about my eyes,' she added. 'Mum says they follow her round and they do.'

Josie confirmed that ever since she'd hung the picture she'd noticed this. She had noticed other strange things as well. One evening when she moved Gail's photograph away from the flower that stood in a vase beside it, the flower promptly wilted.

'It was the weirdest thing,' said Josie. 'I moved the photo on to the chair beside me and a couple of minutes later my husband said, "Look at that flower!" And it had drooped right over. Just out of interest I moved the photo back and after a minute or two the flower recovered.'

It was clear that Gail still took a lively interest in her family and wanted them to know that she wasn't far away. She had even appeared a couple of times.

'I haven't seen her,' said Josie sadly. 'I wish I had but on the day before the funeral her friend told me, "Gail's been to me." And I said, "What?" It sounded so peculiar, but she insisted she wasn't imagining things. "She's crying lots and lots of tears," she said, "because you are all remembering her but not the baby."

'And one night later her grandmother saw her. Apparently she asked, "Who's this woman who's having our dogs? You'd better tell her she'd better look after them properly." '

I was not surprised that Gail was so concerned for her family when I realized who she was and the horrifying circumstances of her death. The name had sounded vaguely familiar and, as the sitting progressed, I realized she was the girl who had been accidentally shot by the police a couple of years ago when her boyfriend used her as a human shield during a raid on his flat.

Many people will remember the case but know little of the events that led up to the nightmare. It was only when Josie told me the whole story after the sitting that I understood why Gail wanted to contact her mother so badly.

'Gail was a real tomboy,' said Josie. 'She was never bothered with the lads. She liked to come out in the evening with her stepfather and me, she was record mad and she loved kids. She and her friend used to go baby-sitting and after a while Gail started baby-sitting for a couple who lived across the road. They had a little boy she was very fond of.'

The arrangement had been going on for some weeks when Josie began to feel uneasy. She discovered the couple weren't married and although she had nothing against David Pagett to start with her husband, Jim, had never liked him and she began to feel the same way.

'He was very smooth and a good talker and at first, when you had no reason to suspect otherwise, you believed what he said,' Josie went on, 'but after a while I realized it was all talk. He couldn't be trusted to tell the truth. The trouble was Gail, being so much younger, only sixteen, and more impressionable, was very vulnerable. She'd never had a proper boyfriend before, she had no experience of men and I suppose, in her eyes, he was wonderful.'

By the time Josie realized they were going out together secretly, it was too late. Gail was in love.

'He was twice her age and he really impressed her. He used to take her out for meals in nice restaurants and he bought her clothes. But there were also odd bruises beginning to appear on her arms. Well, of course, I didn't like it at all and I tackled Gail about it. We can both be a bit fiery. There was a row and I said, "If you don't stop seeing him you can pack your bags and go." It was just one of those things you say. I never dreamed she'd actually leave – but she did.'

David Pagett's common-law wife had walked out in disgust when she discovered the affair, leaving Pagett with their son.

'He wanted Gail to move in and look after the boy and she was quite happy to. She was very fond of them both,' said Josie. 'I couldn't stop her. I went to the police, I went

29

to the social services, but they said they couldn't do anything about it. Gail was over the age of consent and she needn't come home unless she wanted to.'

As the weeks went by it became clear that the relationship was going wrong. Neighbours told Josie of violent rows between the couple and when she saw Gail, the girl was usually bruised.

'I tried to persuade her to come home, but she never would. One day as I was going out I saw a car pull up opposite and Gail got out, crying and covered in bruises. "Why don't you come home, love?" I asked. "What's this hold he's got over you?" And she said, "You don't know what he's like, mum." And apparently on the night it happened Gail told her friend Marie that he had said, "If you go home I'll get your mum." And she really believed he would kill me if she left him.'

Despite his threats Pagett obviously still feared Josie's influence over her daughter because he suddenly moved his little family to a flat on the other side of Birmingham, well away from Gail's old home. But the contact was not broken. When Pagett was out Gail often phoned her mother and Josie, who had her own car, visited Gail whenever the coast was clear. One day, however, to her surprise, she found Pagett at home and apparently in a civil mood.

'He seemed really pleased with himself,' said Josie. ' "I think you ought to know she's pregnant," he told me. I'm quite sure he got her pregnant deliberately because he thought it would make me disown her. I must admit I was shocked but I was determined he wouldn't see it. "Good," I snapped, "because it won't be born in this hole." Later I told Gail I thought she had more sense but I wasn't really cross. How can you be angry about a new grandchild on the way?

'But I became more and more worried. Gail wasn't

going to ante-natal classes because Pagett didn't want anyone to see her bruises. One day his sister came round and said to me, "You've got to get that girl away from him. He'll kill her."

' "Gail, that baby will be born with something wrong with it," I used to plead, but still she wouldn't budge, although I knew she wasn't happy.

'Then one day she rang me and said she couldn't take any more. "Right," I said, "I'm coming to fetch you now."

' "But I can't leave, they've left me baby-sitting," she said.

"Timmy's all right, he's asleep, isn't he?" I said. "I'm getting my coat on and I'll be right over."

'I drove to the flat as fast as I could and when Gail opened the door she was shaking. She hurried to the car and I made the return journey even faster than the outward one. She was still shivering when we got indoors so I ran her a bath and as she climbed in I was shocked to see that you couldn't put a finger between the bruises that covered her body. She was black and blue all over.'

Josie hoped that now Gail was away from her boyfriend the worst was over and at first it looked as if she was right.

'He was very angry when he found out and he was on the phone every night arguing. We wouldn't let him speak to Gail and Jim, my husband, told him to keep away from the house or he'd break his neck. But Gail seemed to settle. We went out and bought everything for the baby, a cot, a bath and a carry cot, everything. She was delighted.

'Then Pagett started phoning during the day while we were at work and I'd come home to find Gail in tears. I spoke to the social worker at the hospital hoping for advice but she only said, "Why can't you compromise? Have her at home, but let her see him."

'I knew that would be a disaster but I certainly didn't want to keep Gail locked up. I encouraged her to go out with her other friends and she did. She seemed to enjoy herself.

'Then one night in June, Jim and I were going to Jim's son's and Gail and her friend were going to stay with the friend's sister. Jim and I dropped them off on our way out and thought no more about it. We must have come home just before midnight which was fairly usual. I went into the living-room to draw the curtains, Jim headed for the kitchen to put the kettle on, when the doorbell rang.

' "I'll go, love," Jim called and went out to answer it. I was just wondering who it could be at that time of night, when there was a great crash. Jim came dashing back, grabbed me and dragged me out into the garden.

' "Quick, he's got a gun!" he yelled.

'But Pagett was right behind us. I turned to see a double-barrelled shot-gun pointing straight at Jim. Without thinking, I lunged forward and wrenched the barrel upwards just as Pagett fired. There was a loud crack and the shot went through Gail's bedroom window. Furiously, Pagett swung round, knocked me down with the butt of the gun and aimed at Jim again, but this time Jim was ready. He leapt towards the garden fence which is four and a half feet high. Another shot rang out and Jim disappeared over the fence.

'There was silence. Had he been hit? Pagett seemed to think so. Was my Jim lying dead in our neighbour's garden?

'There was no time to find out. Blood was pouring from my head but Pagett dragged me up by my hair and marched me out to his car. "Right, you bastard!" he shouted. "Where's your daughter hiding?"

'I wouldn't tell him. I couldn't if I'd wanted to. My mouth was as dry as a desert. But he kept threatening to shoot me if I didn't answer. He had probably already killed Jim so I didn't doubt that he meant what he said. In the end I gave him the address of another friend of Gail's. I thought he might go there which would give me time to phone the police, but no. He pushed me into the car and took me with him.

' "It better not be the wrong flat, that's all," he snarled.

'Well, of course it was, but the girl who answered the door told him the truth. She didn't have much choice. I got another clout but I didn't mind because I thought at least the girl would have the sense to phone Gail and warn her that we were on the way.

'Well, she did, but unfortunately Gail had hysterics when she heard. Her friends told her to go and hide but she wouldn't.

' "He's got my mum! He's got my mum! He'll kill her," she kept sobbing and she refused to move.

'In the meantime Pagett was driving like a maniac and we got to the flat just as the other girl's boyfriend was arriving. Pagett called out "John!" all friendly, and when the girls opened the door to John, who they thought would be able to look after them, we were right behind him.

'Inside the flat Pagett covered us all with the gun.

' "Get over here," he ordered Gail, but she had seen my head was bleeding.

' "What have you done to my mum?"

'He hit her, knocked me in the ribs with the gun to prevent me going to her aid and threw her down the stairs. She was six months' pregnant. Then he dragged me down after her and pushed us both into the car. There wasn't much room because Gail was quite big by now, but she sat on my lap. Pagett jumped into the driver's seat, swung the car round and it was obvious he was heading back to his flat. He was driving like a lunatic and all the time he was hitting Gail in the face with his free hand. I was trying to protect her and wondering what on earth we could do. I thought if I grab the steering wheel she'll go straight through the windscreen.

'Then I looked back and saw a police car in the distance. I had no idea whether it was just a coincidence or whether they were looking for us, but Pagett saw it too.

' "I'm going to stop and you can drive," he said. Whether he thought they might be looking for a car with a man at the wheel and would be thrown off the scent if I was driving, or whether he simply wanted his hands free to shoot at them if they got too close, I didn't know, but I thought this was our chance of escape. I agreed and he stopped the car. Obediently I opened the door then I pushed Gail out as hard as I could and she ran into the street shouting for help.

' "He's got a gun! He's going to kill us!"

'Pagett was taken by surprise and, while he was off guard, I grabbed his hair and banged his head against the windscreen as hard as I could. I wanted to knock him out but it didn't even seem to hurt him. He twisted round in rage, threw me out of the car and leapt out after me with the gun in his hand.

'I was sure then that I was finished. He stood over me with the barrel of the gun inches from my head, his finger on the trigger. Then I heard Gail's voice.

' "Don't do it! Don't shoot! I'll do anything, anything you say, only please don't shoot!"

'To my surprise he hesitated, then lowered the gun and pushed Gail back into the car. The engine started and they raced away leaving me on the ground.

'I was really frantic then. I was terrified of what he

would do to Gail when he got her back to his flat. I jumped up and, as I stepped into the road, I saw a kid on a motor-bike coming along. The poor boy must have thought I was mad. I flagged him down, said "Follow that car!" just like they do in films, and climbed on the back. He wasn't at all happy about it but I don't think he dared disobey me.'

After a short distance Josie flagged down a passing car and they took her to the police station, then to the flat.

'The flat was surrounded by police when we got there and there was an ambulance standing by. "You'd better go in the ambulance," someone said and I thought they were worried about the wound on my head. But that obviously wasn't the idea at all. They locked me in. So that I wouldn't panic or get in the way, I suppose. For two hours I sat there chewing my nails in agony of fear and frustration. Then I heard movement outside.

' "The marksmen have arrived," said the ambulance driver cheerfully, thinking I'd be better for a progress report.

'I was horrified. "Oh, my God."

' "It's all right, they won't shoot," he reassured me but, even before he'd finished speaking, shots rang out.

'The ambulance doors opened and I burst out just in time to see Gail being carried from the flat on a stretcher. "Give me a gun and I'll kill the bastard!" I shouted as I ran to Gail. But I was crying and holding her hand and I knew I couldn't leave her.'

At the hospital, Josie was told that the baby was dead, Gail's chances of survival were slim, and that her husband, Jim, was alive but he might lose his leg. Pagett had wounded him in the thigh.

Gail died a month later. Pagett was sentenced to twelve years' imprisonment.

As Josie finished her terrible story you could have

heard a pin drop in the room. How she had kept sane these past two years I couldn't imagine. Sometimes I wonder what on earth is happening to the world, there seems to be so much violence. But at least knowing the background now helped to put the sitting into perspective. One thing that had puzzled me was the way Gail refused to talk about her boyfriend.

'Him!' she'd said emphatically, 'I don't even want to think about him.' She wouldn't even mention his name. I found that odd at the time but, after hearing Josie's story, the reason became clear. Gail loved her family very much and she was distressed at the misery David Pagett had brought them.

She had come through immediately I tuned in and I realized that she was quite a character. She was eager to communicate and very forthright.

'Isn't my mum smart?' she asked me, drawing attention to Josie's immaculate blue suit, shoes and handbag.

Gail wanted to reassure her mother she was all right. Then she said, 'I was so stupid, Doris. Can you forgive me, Mum? I'm very stubborn and the more they talk at me the more I go the other way. That was my biggest fault. My mother could see it wasn't right and she tried to take me out of it, but I wouldn't listen. Instead, my life was thrown away and he wasn't even free. I've found that out since. My mother wasn't even angered about the baby. She wanted the baby. Mum and Dad had bought me everything for my baby. Even the cot.'

Gail mentioned some family names and asked particularly to be remembered to a girl named Barbara who used to work with her.

Then she sighed and the power wavered. 'It's bloody hard work this, isn't it, Doris?'

'Yes, it is, love,' I agreed laughing. Gail clearly hadn't changed a bit. She'd never been a saint on the earth plane and there was no reason to become saintly on the other side. But she was right. Communicating is difficult for spirit people, particularly the first time they try it.

'You see, I wanted to come home but he wouldn't let me,' she went on. 'He was a swine and I was the only one who couldn't see it, but I saw it that night and all I wanted to do was come home. Me and my baby. And if I had to come over why couldn't it have happened straight away? But they thought I was getting better, that was the awful part. Why couldn't I have come over with the baby? He went first and I lived on for nearly a month.'

Josie confirmed that this was right. There were more family details, then Gail told me that Josie had kept one of her rings.

Josie said this was true and spread out her fingers. She wore several rings on each hand and I wondered which one was Gail's.

'No, it's not one of those,' said Gail's voice loudly in my ear. 'She's not wearing it. There's another one and she's not got it on.'

It turned out that Josie had brought with her the cheap little 'engagement' ring Pagett had given Gail. She couldn't bring herself to wear it and on the way to see me she'd almost flung it in a rubbish bin, but at the last minute the thought struck her that it might help the communication and so she slipped it into her handbag.

Gail chattered on, describing the place where her mother worked and the health problems of one of her colleagues. Then she said, 'Give Eric a big hug for me. I miss him. I miss you all.'

I wondered who Eric could be, since Josie had said her husband's name was Jim, but it turned out that Eric and Jim were one and the same person.

'She's the only one who used to call him Eric,' Josie explained.

I kept hearing something about a motor-bike, too, but I couldn't make out what Gail was talking about. It was only afterwards when Josie mentioned flagging down a bike to help her follow Pagett's car that I realized Gail must have been trying to tell me something about that night.

She was very concerned about proving to her mother that she still visited the house and was interested in the family. She told me about that unusual picture on the wall, about a new baby recently born, and the birthday of her little nephew Adam. She even tried to tell me the name of the street where her mother lived but I couldn't catch it. It was just a mumble.

'Come on, Doris, think of trees,' she said in exasperation. But it was no use. 'Oak? Elm?' I tried. She laughed and shook her head.

Afterwards I discovered it was 'wood' – Brandwood. She also insisted that Josie had put something in her coffin with her but Josie denied this.

'It wouldn't have been a flower or anything, would it?' I suggested, but Josie said no. There was nothing. It was only a few weeks later that she remembered the promise she had made as Gail lay dying.

'She was unconscious and all wired up to drips and things,' said Josie. 'They said she wouldn't last much longer. I climbed on the bed beside her and took her in my arms and even though I knew she couldn't hear me I promised she wouldn't be parted from her baby. And she wasn't. When she died, I had the baby put in the coffin with her.'

It was two years since she'd passed but Gail was still worried about her mother. 'I come and see her at night,' she said, 'and I sit on the bed. She can't sleep. When she closes her eyes she sees that night all over again like a film.'

This really amazed Josie. 'Yes, that's right. When I try to sleep I can't remember nice things any more. It's just that night over and over again, every night. I see every detail in my mind just as if I'm watching a picture on a screen.'

Gail was getting tired now and her voice was fading away but, before she finished, her face, surrounded by a swinging curtain of dark hair, appeared beside her mother's and she said, 'Tell Mum I've got Daniel with me,' and in the last flash of power I had a glimpse of a beautiful toddler with bright auburn hair.

'She says she's got Daniel with her,' I told Josie, and at that she crumbled.

She hurried out of the room to compose herself but when she returned she looked a lot better.

'That's what I was waiting for, Doris,' she said. 'Only Gail and I knew that if the baby was a boy she was going to call him Daniel.'

Well, of course the baby was a boy, and though he was never born on earth, he was growing up with his mum in the spirit world and he was now a little toddler of two.

And Gail, true to her word, had named him Daniel.

# CHAPTER 3

All my life I have been surrounded by children, earth children and spirit children, it makes no difference to me. The only sad thing about spirit children as far as I'm concerned is that, although I can see them, I can't cuddle them or spoil them with sweets. Apart from that they are children like other children.

A few years ago one or two parents started giving me snapshots of their little ones after they'd had a sitting with me. 'I'd like her to stay here with you and John Michael,' they'd say and naturally I would put up the pictures next to the only photograph that was ever taken of our son. Of course, as the months went on other parents would notice the pictures and that would prompt further snaps, until today I have so many photographs I've had to mount them on a special cork board and the way things are going I shall need another board very soon.

I know each of them by name, I try to remember their birthdays and, probably because I have no grandchildren of my own, I like to think of them as my spirit grandchildren. Call me daft if you like, I don't care. They are individuals to me, they have been to my flat to talk and, if they have a message for their parents, they know they can come back and mention it to me whenever they like and I will pass it on.

I try to give them fresh flowers every week, at Christmas I put a tiny tinsel Christmas tree on the shelf for them and when I'm going away I tell them, 'I won't be seeing you for a few days. I'm going to Manchester (or wherever) so I won't see you unless you'd like to come with me.'

40

And this book is for them, that's why it's called *Innocent Voices In My Ear.* Oh, I know some of them get into bad ways and do silly things that they regret afterwards, but underneath they're still innocent children. There's little Robert who had a tumour on the brain, two-year-old Martin Vosper who was killed by falling scaffolding, baby Oliver Thomas who was shaken so violently he died of brain damage, there's Lilian who made a mistake trying to frighten her parents, there's Careen who took her own life, her sister Charmain who died in a road accident, there's Paul who was killed in a motor-cycle crash and Sandy and Mark and Jonathan and, well, I could go on and on. The important thing is that they're all innocent children growing up strong and happy in the spirit world.

What strikes you forcibly when you look at my kids, and visitors often remark on it, is how beautiful they are. Every single one of them is the sort of child you'd notice in a crowd.

'It's always the best ones who die young,' these visitors often add, and unconsciously I think they have hit on the truth.

Time and time again I hear bereaved parents saying the same things. If they've lost a baby it was no ordinary baby. It never cried, it was no trouble, it would go to anyone, it was unusually forward. Older children are always described as being particularly bright, full of life and somehow extra-lovable. The teenagers are always the kind, unselfish ones who attract friends wherever they go. No one pretends these children were angels, they all had their bad moments, but every parent will say that the child who died was special and somehow unlike the other children in the family.

Now, of course I realize that in these circumstances parents are naturally biased, but often their view is confirmed by people outside the family and it's more than coincidence to hear the identical characteristics attributed to children who have nothing else in common except an early death.

Every time I look at my kids I'm reminded of this and I've come to the conclusion that they are God's special children. They are old souls who don't need to spend much time on earth. They have their useful purpose to fulfil and when they've done their job they have to return to the spirit world. I like to think that the parents of these children, and I'm one of them, have been specially chosen for the task and that we should be thankful that we were allowed to have them, if only for a little while.

I mustn't give the impression that my sitting-room is open *only* to spirit children. There are photographs of living children dotted about all over the place, too, and I've known some pretty special earth children over the years.

As a child, I dreamed of a nursing career but, after my father died, my mother couldn't afford to let me stay on at school and my education wasn't good enough for medicine. Instead, I worked for a time as a ward maid in a large hospital but it wasn't the same. Mother wanted me home and I decided that if I couldn't be a nurse I wanted to be a children's nanny.

Unfortunately, even that seemed impossible. It was a responsible position and you needed experience. How a girl of fourteen going on fifteen gained the necessary experience I had no idea. Neither had Mother but, in her practical way, she told me to put such notions out of my head and get on with the work I *could* do. I was a strong healthy girl, so I was sent to various houses in Grantham to act as a general dogsbody.

In her heart of hearts, though, Mother must have felt this wasn't good enough because, after only a few months, she was not only prepared to listen to an alternative, she actually allowed it.

One day the relative of a neighbour of ours, Mrs Anthony, came to see her. Mrs Anthony had just accepted the position of housekeeper in a household in Bournemouth and she was looking for a maid to take with her.

'Now, your Doris is just the sort of girl I'm looking for,' she told Mother. 'She's wasted here. In Bournemouth she would be working in a properly run household, she'd wear a uniform and she'd learn how to conduct herself. She'd become a properly trained maid. With that experience behind her she could go anywhere.'

Mother was impressed, but *Bournemouth*? It seemed like the other side of the world. She didn't think she could let me go so far away. After all I was only fifteen.

Here Mrs Anthony played her trump card. 'But Doris is a sensible girl, very grown up for her age,' she said. 'And, besides, I would be with her. I would take care of her.'

The next thing I knew I was off to Bournemouth. I was very excited. There were two new uniforms in my case, a print dress for the mornings and a black dress with a little white apron and cap for the afternoons. I wasn't quite sure why you had to change twice in one day but Mrs Anthony assured me that it was the right thing to do.

'They do things properly in Bournemouth,' she said. 'It's a very genteel place.'

I took that to mean posh and was even more excited.

As the steam train chugged away the miles to the south coast I tried very hard not to wriggle in my seat. Mrs Anthony had said I was very grown up for my age and I was determined not to let her down.

'Now, you just behave yourself for Mrs Anthony, our Doris,' Mother had said as I left, 'or she'll send you home.'

I didn't want to go home. I was going to live by the sea in Bournemouth in a grand house owned by posh people and in a year or two I was bound to work my way up to the position of nanny. Such things happened, I was sure of it.

I don't know what I'd been expecting – some sort of stately home perhaps – but at the first sight of the house my hopes came crashing down. It was a dark gloomy place and the sea could have been fifty miles away for all you could see of it. Across the road was a forest of brooding pine trees and the pungent scent seemed to fill your nostrils wherever you went. At night, as I lay in my tiny attic bedroom, I could hear the wind tearing through the tree tops and the branches creaking, and when the gales blew in from the sea I was sure I'd wake up to find a fallen pine completely blocking the street.

One day in my new job was enough to convince me that my dreams of working my way up to nanny were hopeless. The master and mistress, a colonel and his lady home from India, seemed pretty old to me and, besides that, the mistress spent all her time in bed. She was an invalid, Mrs Anthony explained. I don't know what was wrong with her but she had a private nurse living in and it was quite obvious that there would be no babies.

I did have a small charge to look after, however – the family parrot. I'd never seen a parrot before, outside picture books that is, and when they introduced me to Christopher I was charmed. He was a magnificent bird with brilliant turquoise feathers splashed with yellow and green. All day long he sat on a perch in the mistress' bedroom, grumbling to himself or preening for visitors, and to look at, he was wonderful.

It was when they explained my duties regarding Christopher that I became apprehensive. Christopher did not spend the night upstairs. At bedtime I was to carry him down to the conservatory and say 'Do your duty, Christopher' before leaving him for the night amongst the potted palms. The next morning I had to carry him back upstairs to his mistress.

It sounded simple enough. But that first night as I approached the perch I noticed what a malicious glint he had in his hard little eyes and how wicked and sharp that cruel curved beak looked. Gingerly, I put out my hand and lifted the perch. There was a loud screech and, quick as a flash, Christopher twisted round to peck my fingers.

Frightened, I dropped the perch.

There was a gentle murmur from across the room. 'It's all right, he won't hurt you. Be firm with him.'

I gritted my teeth and tried again. The same thing happened.

'Now, do hurry up, dear,' said the mistress, sighing. 'He can't stay here all night.'

I scowled at the parrot and the parrot scowled back. It was no use. I had to get him to the conservatory even if I was bitten to death in the process. I took a deep breath, seized the perch, and raced for the door before I could change my mind. All the way down the back stairs (servants weren't allowed to use the front ones) he squawked, flapped and nipped at my hand in protest, but we reached the conservatory intact.

'Right, do your duty, Christopher!' I hissed from a safe distance and banged the door on him.

It was the beginning of a twice-daily battle. I was scared to death of that parrot and I can only assume the parrot was scared to death of going up and down stairs.

My other duties were easier but not much fun. I got up at six o'clock and cleaned all the grates and lit all the fires before the rest of the household rose. Then I was on call for cleaning and polishing and helping Cook with the vegetables, and at tea time I took a tray up to the mistress.

All the time I was learning how to behave properly and trying to carry out the instructions of Mrs Anthony.

I didn't always succeed. One afternoon I was hurrying down the back stairs with the tea tray when the heel came off my shoe. I slipped, the tray flew out of my hands and the china tea things went crashing to the bottom and smashed to pieces on the hall floor.

The silence that followed was awe-inspiring but not long-lasting. Mrs Anthony came running down the passage.

'Doris, whatever have you done?' Then she saw the broken china. 'Oh, you clumsy girl.'

I came limping down the rest of the stairs. 'The heel came off my shoe,' I explained, holding out the culprit, but Mrs Anthony was already on her knees collecting pieces of china.

'Come on, get this cleared up before the mistress wonders what's going on.'

But Mrs Anthony wasn't really cross and I soon discovered why. A little later she called me to her.

'Well, Doris, I must say goodbye,' she said briskly.

My mouth fell open. 'Why, are you going out?'

'No, I'm taking up a new position.'

'A *new* position?' I gasped. 'But what about this one? What about me?'

'You?' She looked surprised. 'Well, you're doing very nicely, dear. As long as you don't have too many accidents like this afternoon's I'm sure the mistress will be well satisfied with you. Just try to remember the things I've taught you.' And with that she went off to pack her things, leaving me speechless.

It didn't stop there. Soon after Mrs Anthony's departure, the cook stopped coming, so I had to cook dinner as well. Luckily, the private nurse was sympathetic.

'You ought to get out more, Doris,' she said, and when

I explained that I'd like to but I had nowhere to go, she mentioned a girls' club nearby.

The discovery of the club transformed my stay in Bournemouth. It was a noisy, friendly place, full of girls my own age, and we made our own entertainment with a round of fancy dress parties, concerts and amateur dramatics.

It was through the club that I moved on to my next job. The woman who ran the place was concerned when she found out about my life. She knew I had to work very hard in that depleted household and she said, 'I don't think it's good for Doris to be there. There's nobody young for her to talk to.' So concerned was she that she helped me find another place.

My dreams of working up to nanny flooded back but, once again, I was out of luck. There was less work in my new job but no chance of children. The mistress was an old lady who was stone deaf and the house was run by her much younger companion, an arty type, tall and very thin with a fluting voice and long, trailing chiffon scarves.

The companion was kind but rather eccentric. She played the piano and she liked to pretend the house belonged to her. In the evenings after she'd got the old lady to bed she used to say to me: 'Go to bed, Doris. I'll bring your supper up.' And she would bring me supper on a tray in bed, purely so that she could have the house to herself.

I didn't mind because, if I wasn't going out, I was happy to read in bed, and if I *was* going out the companion didn't mind because she had the house to herself anyway. We got along quite well and, being arty, she took an interest in the theatrical projects of the club. She even helped me make my fancy dress costumes.

After that uneasy start I found I was enjoying Bournemouth very much and I was quite settled when the letter from Mother came. Poor Mother, she could never make up her mind what to do with me. She would send me away to a distant job with what she considered to be good prospects only to find she was lonely without me and wanted me back again. This happened several times and it happened in Bournemouth. I was needed at home, she wrote, she enclosed the fare and I was to come back as soon as I could.

Reluctantly I said goodbye to my new friends and headed north. I wasn't very happy. It seemed I was back where I started when Mrs Anthony had called on Mother. I was no nearer achieving my ambitions. Or so I thought.

Oddly enough as it turned out, I was closer than I'd ever been.

Mother had found me a job at a place called Harrowby Hall. I'm not quite sure what it was, possibly some sort of government training scheme, but there were men from all over the country staying there and this meant an enormous amount of cooking. I was to help the cook as kitchen maid. The potato peeling, vegetable chopping and washing up seemed endless, but people often dropped in for a chat and the hours passed quite quickly.

A local man called Commander Pesani was a frequent caller and one day I heard him talking to the housekeeper.

'So we're desperate for somebody who loves children to come and help out,' he was saying.

The housekeeper nodded sympathetically, then she caught sight of me. 'It's a pity we can't do without Doris,' she said. 'She adores children.'

'Yes, I do,' I added wistfully and, as I walked away, I felt the Commander's eyes on my back.

Later that day as I was taking some rubbish out to the bins I was surprised to see that Commander Pesani hadn't left. He walked quickly across the courtyard.

'Do you really love children?'

'Oh yes, more than anything.'

'And do you think you would like to help out in our nursery?'

I nodded.

'Well, look, come and see Mrs Pesani next week and we'll see what can be arranged.' Quickly, he handed me his card and then hurried away as if afraid the house-keeper would catch him.

And that's how my happy days at The Red House in Melton Mowbray began. The Red House was a large red brick building set in beautiful grounds and when I went to see Mrs Pesani she explained that they were looking for a nurserymaid to assist their nanny. There were three children, Vivienne (five), John (four) and baby Patrick, and they wanted someone to live in, in a room close to the night nursery. It sounded marvellous to me and I was sure I could get Mother to agree. After all, compared with Bournemouth, Melton Mowbray was just down the road.

Once again I was fitted out with a smart uniform, a brown dress trimmed in cream with a cream apron, and I set off eagerly to my new life.

Nanny was rather forbidding at first: a thin, prim woman in a smart uniform with a veil down the back of her hat. She was very strict, she told me, and didn't stand any nonsense.

'And I won't allow spoiling in my nursery,' she added sternly, obviously suspecting a weakness in that direction. Rightly, as it turned out.

The children were lovely. Vivienne was a pretty girl with dark, almost black, hair and eyes, John was slim and sensitive-looking with soft wavy hair, while Patrick was a fat, good-tempered baby, a lazy child who would sooner laugh than cry.

The two boys slept in the night nursery, Nanny slept in

the room next door, Vivienne in a room on the same landing, and my room was just down the corridor. The day nursery was downstairs and had its own little kitchen and the children's toys – and they had just about every toy imaginable – were kept in an outhouse in the grounds.

The children visited their parents once a week for lunch on Sundays and they said goodnight to them at bedtime. They also saw their mother on Nanny's day off when she helped me bathe them. Apart from that they spent their time with Nanny and me.

My duties were fairly simple. After Christopher the parrot, I reckoned I could cope with most things. I cleaned the nursery, made the beds and mended clothes. I also cooked light meals. Food in the nursery was very plain. The children always had to eat their bread and butter before they were allowed anything more exotic and they only had fancy cakes on birthdays. There was a lot of Marmite on toast and boiled eggs with soldiers and sometimes if they'd had a light tea they were allowed milk and a plain biscuit which was a great treat. Their teeth were absolutely perfect and they had beautiful skins as a result of this diet.

As Nanny had instinctively known, I was a spoiler. If the baby was crying I couldn't resist going to see what was wrong with him. 'What's the matter, darling?' I'd ask, despite Nanny's warnings that he only did it to get attention. And sometimes when the children came out all warm and pink from their baths I'd let them come down to the day nursery in their dressing gowns and give them a biscuit. Of course if Nanny found out I got my head in a sling.

'Dose, will you *not* do that,' she'd say, folding her lips into a thin line.

They all called me Dose. I managed to get through my chores each day so that I had a lot of time left for playing with the children. I used to crawl around the floor with them like a big kid myself. I would get down on all fours so they could ride on my back or we would play hospitals and they would bandage me until I looked like the Invisible Man. They were also very fond of playing shops and I let them take the food out of the pantry and arrange it on the table in front of whoever was shopkeeper. Then we set up a little bell for the customer to ring as he came through the 'door' to make his purchase.

John took this game very seriously as I discovered later when I took him to the children's harvest festival service at the church.

John had never been to a proper church service before and he watched in fascination as the vicar, followed by the choir boys, walked in procession towards the altar. His eyes grew rounder and rounder and when the vicar climbed up into the pulpit his mouth dropped open. Silence fell over the congregation. The vicar took a deep breath and was just about to start the service when a clear piping voice which carried beautifully through the old stone building said, 'Oh, Dosey, isn't the vicar *rude*! He's got up there with his feeder on!'

Heads turned, there were stifled giggles, and the vicar didn't look too amused. Blushing scarlet, I shushed John and with a sour little smile the vicar opened the service. But John hadn't finished with the vicar yet.

The children's harvest festival was a pretty affair. The church was filled with flowers, and small children clutching baskets of fruit and vegetables packed the aisles. The highlight of the service came when the children filed to the altar to present their offerings to the vicar.

I explained all this to Vivienne and John, adding, 'And afterwards the offerings are taken to the hospital for the sick people to enjoy.'

They seemed to understand and, when the moment

came, Vivienne, being the eldest, went first. She used to go to dancing classes and, inspired by her last lesson, she handed over her basket with a charming little curtsey. Everyone smiled and there were murmurs of 'Dear little girl!' I swelled with pride. That was *my* little girl they were talking about. Then came John. He strode towards the vicar, thrust out his basket and then stood there with his legs apart, hands behind his back like a miniature version of his father. The vicar looked a bit puzzled and said something to him but John didn't move.

'John!' I called softly. 'John!'

He didn't budge.

'John. Come back to Dose, John!'

'But he hasn't given me any shillings for it yet,' John wailed for all to hear.

As he knew very well from our games of shop, when a customer was given a basket of food, the shopkeeper was given a handful of 'shillings' in return.

They were well-behaved children generally but, like all children, they loved a joke. Nanny was a bit strict and they weren't sure how she would react to their fun, but the minute her back was turned they were up to their pranks with me.

There was a little table with matching chairs in the nursery kitchen and the seats came out of the chairs for easy cleaning. One of the children's favourite tricks was to remove the seats from my chair and then call me for 'tea'.

'Dose, tea's ready!' they'd call and I would come in and say:

'Where am I to sit?'

Bursting with laughter they'd pull out a chair, spluttering, 'Sit here, Dose, sit here!'

And of course, pretending not to notice the missing seat, I'd sit down and my bottom would go right through.

52

They found this so funny they'd roll about on the floor laughing and laughing. But one day this harmless game almost got us into trouble. I went straight through the chair in the normal way, but this time, being rather plump and perhaps sitting down more heavily than usual, I got stuck. Try as I would, I couldn't get out and when I stood up the chair came with me.

The children found this hysterically funny.

'Come on, you've got to help,' I told them. 'Push, push Dose's bottom.'

Well, they tried but they were laughing so much they didn't do any good and I found I was laughing, too. It seemed to get funnier and funnier and in the end we made so much noise Mrs Pesani came in to see what was going on.

She stood in the doorway, looking from the hysterical children rolling on the floor to me with my behind stuck through the chair, and for one awful moment I thought she was going to explode with anger.

Then her lips started to twitch and she began to laugh.

'You look as if you need some help, Dose.'

I breathed a sigh of relief. It was all right, she wouldn't tell Nanny. I would be in trouble if she did that.

No, the children were rarely naughty but they often got themselves into trouble with Nanny for thoughtless behaviour, particularly if it involved getting dirty.

One afternoon they were going to a party and we'd got them washed and changed and ready to go and Nanny sent them down to wait in the garden while she prepared herself.

I was racing round collecting up the discarded clothes and tidying the nursery before we left, because Nanny couldn't bear to walk out on a disorderly nursery, when something made me go to the window. It was too quiet, I suppose, and I was wondering what they were getting

53

up to. I don't know what I'd expected to see: Vivienne sitting on the grass in her party dress perhaps, or John making mud pies. But the reality was worse than I'd imagined.

There was John with a rusty old kettle in his hand, which he'd obviously filled with pebbles from the drive, standing on tiptoe pouring a stream of little stones on to baby Patrick's head.

Patrick, cheerful as ever, didn't seem to mind. He just sat in his pram smiling away as the pebbles piled up on his clean new bonnet, which by now would be filthy, to say nothing of the condition of John's hands and trousers.

Horrified, I threw open the window.

'John, what *do* you think you're doing?'

Startled, he looked up at me and then down at his brother as if noticing him for the first time. Then he patted him on the head, scattering pebbles all over the pram.

'I'm sorry, but I thought you were the tea-pot, darling!' he said.

How could I be cross? I rushed downstairs with a new bonnet for Patrick and a damp cloth to wipe John's hands, but I couldn't scold him.

John was probably the most imaginative of the three and it was difficult to keep up with him at times. He had a topsy-turvy way of looking at things which was quite logical, as long as you understood his logic.

The Pesanis rented a seaside house in Clacton for a month in the summer and one year, after a glorious holiday on the shore, John, Vivienne and I were driving home with the luggage. It was quite late at night, the sky was dark and the moon was hazy with mist the way it is when it's going to rain.

The children were quiet in the back and I was just thinking they must be asleep when John spoke.

'Look, Viv,' he said, 'there's God in bed.'

Vivienne peered out of the window.

'Don't be stupid,' she said scornfully, 'I can't see God in bed.'

'Dosey, you can see God in bed, can't you?' he appealed to me.

I looked out but, much as I would have liked to, I couldn't see a thing that in any way resembled God in bed.

'No, I'm afraid I can't, John,' I admitted.

Impatiently, John craned his head out of the window and looked up at the moon.

'You are stupid,' he said in disgust. 'Can't you see his bedside light?'

Most children are psychic until the ages of eleven or twelve when the world intrudes, and I looked for signs of it in my young charges. At the time, of course, I didn't know the word to describe the quality I was looking for, and I didn't realize how common it was. I only remembered that when I was about Vivienne's and John's age I had several playmates nobody else could see and I half expected Vivienne and John to have some.

If they did, they never mentioned them to me and never gave any sign that there was more going on in the nursery than Nanny and I were aware of. At the time I decided that this was further proof of my own 'peculiarity'. It was years later that I realized Vivienne and John had no need of spirit friends because they had each other and were never lonely. Invisible friends tend to turn up to play with solitary children, particularly children who have lost a brother or sister.

I was alone a lot as a child and my mother had almost died as a result of a fallopian pregnancy, so I did have a spirit brother or sister growing up on the other side. Our adopted son Terry was in a similar position.

He was an 'only' child to us because we'd lost John Michael and all my subsequent pregnancies ended in miscarriage. As a small boy Terry spent a lot of time on his own, except he wasn't alone. Often when he was playing in his room I'd hear all kinds of thumps and bumps through the wall, sounding for all the world like two boisterous boys having a game. Over the top of it would come Terry's voice:

'Give that to me, John Michael. You played with that yesterday.'

In the summer he spent long hours on the lawn with the toy sword John had made for his 'sword fighting'. He was quite alone, yet if you watched him for a moment or two you realized he wasn't alone. He was aiming blows and receiving blows and concentrating on a fixed spot, just as if he was fighting another boy who could not be seen by us.

I was always very careful not to make a fuss about this or behave as if I thought it was in any way unusual. I knew what I had gone through as a child, forever nagged and hounded for being 'strange', and I was determined Terry shouldn't suffer in the same way. After all there's nothing odd about it, it's perfectly natural.

I was reminded of this when a neighbour in Grantham mentioned that she was having similar problems with her small daughter.

'My mother-in-law says I must do something about Claire,' she sighed. 'She says it's not natural.'

'What's the matter with Claire? She looks perfectly well to me,' I said, for Claire was a picture of glowing health, an apparently happy, well-balanced little girl.

56

'Yes, but she's got this friend called Roger,' said her mother.

'Oh, and where does Roger live?'

'That's just it. Roger doesn't live anywhere. He's an invisible Roger.'

It all became clear. 'Oh, one of those.'

She looked put out. 'What d'you mean, one of those?'

'One of the spirit children,' I explained. 'Have you ever lost a baby?'

'No,' she said. 'Never.'

'Well, did you ever have a miscarriage?'

She thought for a moment. 'Yes, I did, at four months.'

'Don't you think it's possible that this could be her brother and she can see him and you can't?' I asked.

She stared at me for a moment as if unable to make up her mind whether I was serious or not.

'Well, you must admit it's pretty far-fetched.' Then she stopped. 'Yet, you know, he seems so real to Claire, I almost think she can see him.'

'Anyway, the child is happy,' I said. 'She's obviously in good health. It's not doing her any harm, so does it matter?'

'Yes, you're quite right,' she said. 'I'll tell my mother-in-law to mind her own business.'

And she did. Before they knew it they were accepting Roger as part of the family even though they couldn't see him. When they were going out in the car, Claire would be strapped in her seat and then she'd say, 'Make room for Roger,' and even her daddy would stand back to let Roger climb in beside her. There were practical advantages, too. Before Roger had come along Claire had been afraid to go upstairs in the dark on her own, but now Roger held her hand and she went upstairs quite happily.

57

I happened to be there one evening at bedtime when this was going on.

'I'd better come up with you, Claire,' said her mother.

'No,' said Claire, 'I'm a big girl now, I can go up on my own.'

'But I'll have to switch out the light when you're in bed,' said her mother. 'You can't reach.'

'It's all right, Roger will do it,' said Claire confidently.

Her mother turned to me in exasperation.

'You see what I mean?'

'Well, never mind, let her be,' I said. 'You can go up and turn it off when she's asleep.'

So we stood at the bottom of the stairs and watched Claire go up. She went into her bedroom, chatting to Roger. She climbed into bed and lay down. And as we stood watching at the foot of the stairs, there was a loud click, and the light went off.

The sequel to this story came years later. On a return visit to Grantham I happened to bump into Claire, now grown up with children of her own.

We chatted for a while then I said:

'Claire, do you remember anything about when you were a little girl?'

She seemed to know what I was getting at.

'About Roger, you mean?'

'Oh, you remember Roger, do you?' I asked.

'Oh yes,' said Claire. 'He was real, you know. I wasn't making him up like everybody thought. It was lovely to have him around. Whenever I was scared I used to say, "Hold my hand, Roger", and he would take my hand and I felt better right away.'

'When did you stop seeing him?'

'I think it must have been when I was about eleven or twelve,' said Claire. 'It wasn't a sudden break. My life

58

became busier and then one day I realized I hadn't seen Roger for a while. I've not seen him since.'

So the world intruded on Claire and Roger when she was twelve years old. But she will see him again one day. When she finally makes the trip to the other side, Roger will be waiting for her, along with her other friends and relatives.

# CHAPTER 4

It was a miserable day. Outside the window the clouds were piled up, grey on grey as far as the eye could see, and the wind whistled through the tower blocks. There were bright flowers on the window-sill and a line of cheerful get-well cards on the table, but today they couldn't lift my spirits.

I was in hospital *again* and it was really getting beyond a joke.

'Surely I've had more than my fair share of ill health,' I grumbled to the spirit world. 'I mean, this is quite ridiculous. I'm either working or ill.'

There was no answer. So they can't even be bothered to reply, I thought crossly.

It was adhesions, or so they said, that had landed me in hospital this time. I needed an operation because of all the other operations I'd had. It sounds crazy, I know, but they assured me it was true. Scar tissue had built up inside my body from past operations and had attached itself to my liver, causing severe pain. In a tricky, time-consuming operation, the surgeon would have to patiently snip it all away and I wasn't looking forward to it one bit.

'Sometimes,' I said out loud to the spirit world, 'I think you've forgotten me.'

There was complete silence from the other side but an unmistakably earth-bound knocking at the door startled me out of my thoughts.

'Come in,' I sighed.

'Hello, Doris,' said my lovely young nurse. 'Here's some more mail for you.'

And she dropped a large envelope on the bed. If the

spirit world had forgotten me it was clear my many friends on this side had not. I was touched by the constant stream of cards, flowers and telephone messages that poured into the hospital, even Michael Aspel sent good wishes over the air during his radio show.

Today, however, in my self-pitying mood even this display of kindness couldn't cheer me. I couldn't be bothered to open another envelope. I haven't got the energy, I was telling myself dramatically, when I noticed that the address was written in the large rounded hand of a child.

Instantly I melted. I hadn't sunk so low that I could disappoint a child, had I?

I ripped open the envelope and pulled out a large red poster, covered with home-made get-well cards and illustrated poems by Katy Beckinsale, eight-year-old daughter of the actor, the late Richard Beckinsale, and her friend Amber.

'To Dear Doris, We hope you will get better,
There's not a lot to say,
We know you can get better,
Tomorrow or today.

Love Katy.'

That was the main card, beautifully coloured in red and green. Next to it on a frilly-edged sheet patterned by a small pair of scissors and decorated with red hearts, Amber had written her poem.

'Oh dear Doris, PLEASE
Call upon my Nanny so fair, her beautiful blue eyes and fleecy white hair,
also my grandad so brave, I hope up in Heaven he doesn't look so grave,

PLEASE call upon my horses so fair their manes and
  tails is as soft as human hair,
Also my Aunty Lidia who I have never seen,
But I have heard her face is like a moon beam,
And so is yours.

With love,
Amber XXXXXXXXXX'

Next to it, Katy, who had obviously read my first book,
had stuck her poem, lavishly illustrated in pink, lavender
and purple.

'Your baby doth lieth in Heaven, his violet eyes look
  down each day,
And in your head of love and tenderness, his heavenly
  voice seems to say,
Mother I wish thee well, and Father and Terry as well,
  Mother please don't be sad, I have only received my
  PROMOTION.'

And as I read these words the tears poured down my
face. The spirit world had not forgotten me, but it took
an eight-year-old child to remind me of the truth.

I first met Katy when her mother Judy came to me for
a sitting. She had seen me on the Russell Harty Show and
wrote to Russell asking if he could put her in touch with
me.

I was a great fan of poor Richard's. I used to laugh and
laugh at his television shows, but I knew nothing at all
about his private life and I was very surprised to find he
had a daughter of Katy's age. Surely he wasn't old
enough?

He assured me he was and there were other surprises
as well. Far from being a jolly, jokey type, he was in fact
very sensitive and concerned. During his lifetime he said

he used to think he was a natural pessimist. He was very sorry to leave his wife, the actress Judy Loe, behind and I could see why. Judy was a beautiful girl and very brave. She smiled and laughed, yet deep down in her eyes the loss was there, even though several years had gone by since Richard passed.

Richard was a very good communicator and he came through easily but he was very sad at first.

'I was so frightened,' he said. 'There was always this great fear, not only the night I passed but before. I thought I was a natural doomsday boy, a real pessimist, but I realize now I must have known.'

The night he fell ill, Judy was in hospital. They wanted another child and she would need an operation to make it possible.

'I was very frightened that night,' said Richard. 'Then I started getting pains in my left arm and in my chest. I rang some friends and they said feel your pulse, but I didn't know what it should have been.'

Later that night he had a heart attack. He was very sad as he talked of those last hours and Judy confirmed that the facts were correct. What's more, later on when she was sorting out his things, she came across several poems and writings that seemed to show that he knew he wouldn't have long to live. She was so moved when she read them that she collected them together and had them published. One short piece seemed to say it all:

*Baby girl widow please take care of my children.*
*Baby girl widow will make my dreams come true.*

When he wrote those words nobody suspected, least of all Richard, that there was something wrong with his heart.

As the sitting went on, however, Richard cheered up. He sent his love to his Judy Sunshine as he called her.

'Judy was my life,' he said. 'Judy and Kate. My only regret is that I couldn't talk to Judy about my fear. I couldn't make her understand.'

Then he mentioned a girl called Sammy, his daughter by his first wife.

'But, my dear, you're not old enough!' I said in surprise, and he laughed.

'Oh yes, I am. But I was very young when I married and it didn't work.'

He wanted particularly to thank Judy.

'Judy, bless her heart, took my daughter into her heart as well as into our home,' he said, 'and Katy is her sister. I'm only sorry I only had two years to know my daughter Samantha properly.'

As he spoke I suddenly saw him quite clearly beside Judy. I'd always had a mental picture of Richard as he was in *Rising Damp* but he looked different now. His face had filled out, his dark hair was much shorter and those deep shadows had gone from under his eyes.

He sent his love to Ronnie Barker, 'my dearest friend' he called him. He mentioned Katy's birthday and he wanted Judy to be happy.

'Walk in sunshine, you and Katy,' he told her. 'I hope one day you will meet someone who can be a loving companion to you and a father to Katy. I'll always be Katy's father but I wouldn't want you to go through the rest of your lives alone.'

He also talked about his mother, Margaret, and, when she got home, Judy must have told her, because soon afterwards Margaret rang me. She introduced herself and we were chatting when suddenly Richard cut in.

'You don't say Margaret, you say "'Ow's our Maggie

then?" ' he told me and when I passed this on, Margaret started to cry.

'That's it,' she said. 'Every time he came home he called out "Ow's our Maggie then?". He never called me anything else.'

Richard stayed very close to his family, particularly to Katy, whom he adored. She was very like him, with the same dark brown eyes that look straight through you and the same perception.

I've noticed before that when there are small children involved, parents who've passed come back frequently to see them and give them a helping hand when necessary. Children of these parents often remark in later years that they always had the feeling their mum or dad was close when they were in trouble, that although they couldn't see their parent, they could feel their presence. This isn't the result of a fertile imagination. It's a real experience.

Parents do come back when their children need them and it makes no difference how humble or exalted that parent was on earth. First and foremost he or she is a parent.

I was reminded of this recently when a sitting with a young girl called Annie suddenly took the most unexpected turn. I'd been introduced to Lee Everett, the healer wife of comedian Kenny Everett, and one afternoon when she came to visit me she brought a friend called Annie.

Afterwards, as they were leaving, I glanced at Annie and suddenly I could see her differently. Instead of the pretty, modern young girl I had seen before I could see great turmoil and confusion.

'My word, you want some sorting out,' I couldn't help saying aloud.

Her jaw dropped and she stared at me in surprise, but Lee said, 'You can say that again, Doris. She does.'

Poor Annie was in a hell of a muddle. She'd got involved in a business project, she'd given up her flat, her job and just about everything she possessed in an effort to get it off the ground, but nothing seemed to be happening and she was drifting from one day to the next not knowing what to do.

She was a nice, kind-hearted girl and I hated to see her in such a state.

'Look, love, I don't know if it will help but would you like a sitting?' I asked. 'Perhaps the spirit people will be able to suggest something.'

Now, as I've said before, I'm not a fortune teller but occasionally the spirit people can see round corners and when one of their loved ones has reached an all-time low they will often let slip just a little of the future to cheer that unfortunate person and help them live through the present. I couldn't promise they'd do it for Annie, but I thought it was worth a try.

The sitting started off in the ordinary way. Annie's brother came through and various members of her family, but in the background I kept hearing a voice say:

'Ask Yoko, ask Yoko.'

Yoko, I thought, that's strange. I only know of one Yoko, Yoko Ono, the Japanese woman who was married to John Lennon. Obviously it was a more common name than I imagined.

Then came the name John Lennard.

'Oh, that's the lawyer who's involved in the business project,' said Annie.

Then another voice interrupted. 'My name is John Lennon.'

I thought I was getting mixed up with John Lennard who was alive and working with Annie, but the new voice was very firm.

'No, I'm John Lennon, I'm over this side,' he insisted.

'She doesn't know me, but my best friend was talking to her on the phone last night. Elton John from New York.'

I repeated this and Annie said, 'Yes. I was talking to Elton last night.'

It turned out that she used to work in the music business and knew Elton John very well, although she'd never met John Lennon.

Nevertheless, John Lennon seemed to know all about Annie's project.

'Why don't they ask Yoko for backing?' he said. 'After all, they named the project after me.'

Annie agreed that this was true. He mentioned a few more details about the business which were confidential, and then he went back to Elton.

'I loved that boy,' he said. 'He's written a song about me you know. It's called Johnny. He played my song all over the world.'

I don't know much about pop music but Annie seemed to think this was pretty accurate. Nevertheless I still wasn't convinced that I was talking to John Lennon. For one thing it didn't sound like him to me. This man had an American accent and I expected John Lennon to sound Liverpudlian.

'Can you give me any proof it's you?' I asked.

'Yoko and I had matching briefs with our initials on,' he said, 'and she has kept four pairs of my solid gold spectacles.'

Then he started talking about a picture with flowers round it and lots of candles, but neither Annie nor I could understand what he meant. It didn't make sense to us.

'D'you mean that Yoko keeps a picture of you with flowers and candles by it?' I asked.

No, he said, that wasn't what he meant at all. He tried to explain again but I couldn't catch it.

'It's no good. I'm sorry, love, clear the vibration and let's try something else.'

It was only later that we solved the puzzle. Apparently, on the anniversary of his death the fans went round Central Park with a flower-decked portrait of John Lennon and they all lit candles.

Next, he showed me the place where he was killed. Instantly a typical New York scene appeared in my mind. Tall buildings and the trees of Central Park nearby. He owned the whole block, he explained.

'And you've been there,' he said.

'Oh no, I don't think so,' I assured him.

'Yes, you have,' he insisted. 'You did a radio programme there.'

And suddenly the picture changed and I saw an image of John and I standing in a magnificent plant-filled hallway waiting for the lift to take us up to the apartment where Lord Fitzgerald and his wife Peggy broadcast their late-night radio show to the wide-awake New Yorkers.

'Oh yes,' I said slowly. 'That was the last time we were in America. So that was your building was it?'

But John Lennon was off again. He seemed a strange boy. He sounded cocky and rather arrogant, I'm afraid, but he was also concerned about helping people. He went back to Annie's project.

'There's plenty of money. I'd like Yoko to back you as long as you devote part of your time to peace.'

I asked him what he was doing on the other side.

'I'm still composing,' he said. 'And I've met two Brians, one who killed himself with drugs and the other who drowned himself in a swimming pool.'

Annie said he must be referring to Brian Epstein, the Beatles' early manager who died of a drug overdose, and Brian Jones of the Rolling Stones who was found dead in his swimming pool.

'What about the man who shot you?' I asked. 'Do you bear him any bitterness?'

John said he didn't. 'After all, he wasn't right in the head, was he?' Then he laughed. 'And if I had to come over I did it the right way, didn't I, in a blaze of publicity!'

He seemed to have a black sense of humour but underneath it he was a caring person.

'There were a lot of things left undone that I should have done,' he said, and his two sons were particularly on his mind.

'I left Yoko you know,' he said, 'but I realized my true happiness lay with my family and I went back.'

He worried that his eldest boy Julian felt unfairly treated.

'He's gone blond now,' he said, 'but the trouble is he thinks he ought to have a lot more and Yoko thinks she's doing the right thing by waiting till he's older.'

And finally he talked about Sean, the younger son. It was clear that Sean had a special place in his heart and he still spent a lot of time close to him.

'I've shown myself to Sean,' he said. 'Sean has seen me.'

Small children are psychic, so it's quite likely that Sean has seen his daddy and he will certainly continue to feel his presence as he grows up.

It's very strange the way so many pop musicians go over young. I know there is a lot of drinking and drug-taking in that profession which would account for some of the deaths, but a surprising number of these young people go over through no fault of their own. John Lennon was murdered, other singers have been killed in plane crashes, electrocuted by their guitars, or like Marc Bolan, been involved in fatal car accidents.

I have done quite a few sittings for the grieving wives, girlfriends and mothers who are left behind in these tragic cases and, from talking to the mothers, I realize that no matter what sort of wild image the young man may have presented to the rest of the world, no matter what sort of bad habits he may have been led into, to his mother he is still her innocent child. Beneath the permissive exterior lies the little boy she always knew.

I realized this when Marc Bolan's mother, Mrs Phyllis Feld, came for a sitting. It was several years since Marc had been killed but I still had a vague recollection of him. Wasn't he the boy with all those long curls down his back and the eye make-up? Being a Jim Reeves fan myself, Marc Bolan wasn't really my cup of tea so I'd never followed his career, but if you'd asked me what he was like I would probably have said that by the look of him he was one of those couldn't-care-less, rebellious types. Which just shows how wrong you can be. When he came back to talk to his mother, I discovered he was a gentle, kind-hearted young man. He had made mistakes, he knew it and he was ready to admit it.

Mrs Feld had written to me asking for a sitting and I booked her for the only day I happened to have free, but it turned out to be a lucky choice.

As soon as I started working Marc came through singing *Happy Birthday*.

'Why is he singing that?' I asked his mother.

'It's his birthday today,' she explained.

'Twenty-nine,' said Marc.

'Is he twenty-nine today?' I asked.

'No,' said Phyllis, 'but he was twenty-nine when he was killed.'

He then went on to mention his little boy, Rolan, and gave his age, and then he talked of Gloria.

'That's Rolan's mother,' said Phyllis.

'My mum's lovely,' Marc went on. 'She has never blamed Gloria for what happened.'

Apparently Gloria was driving the car the night the accident happened. The Mini went out of control, hit a tree and Marc was killed.

'Gloria was all right,' Marc explained. 'She wasn't unconscious or anything. She kept saying, "Wake up! Wake up, Marc!" But I'd already gone. I think a tyre burst.'

Then, for some reason, he started singing again. This time it was a jolly song called *Tie a Yellow Ribbon Round the Old Oak Tree*, which I found an odd choice. I mean, I'm fond of the song but from the little I knew of Marc's work I didn't think this was his sort of music at all. When he finished the chorus, he muttered something about a girl coming from America on his birthday and tying a ribbon round a tree.

It was double Dutch to Phyllis and me. We couldn't make head nor tail of it.

'We don't know what you mean, love.'

He repeated the message several times but it was no use.

'Let's come back to it later,' I suggested. 'We're not getting anywhere at the moment.'

But a few days later the meaning became clearer. There was a story in the paper about Marc Bolan and it mentioned that his fans still make a pilgrimage every year to the tree where he died. It didn't specifically mention the American girl but since he had a lot of American fans the chances are that an American girl was amongst them.

Marc went on to talk about another Mark. 'But it's his real name,' he said, 'spelt M-A-R-K.' It was only then that I realized Marc didn't spell his own name the same way.

'He has a cousin called Mark,' said Phyllis.

He mentioned other family names and birthdays. Then he gave the name Grace.

71

Phyllis shook her head. 'I don't know anyone called Grace.'

'No, Mum doesn't know her,' said Marc, 'but tell her I've met Elvis Presley and his mother Grace over here.'

Phyllis didn't think this was unlikely. 'Oh yes, he adored Elvis Presley,' she said. 'He would have wanted to meet him.'

Marc added that his mother was soon going to Los Angeles (which was correct) and Elvis wanted her to phone someone called Prissy and give his love to Lisa.

'Elvis' wife was called Priscilla,' said Phyllis, 'and his daughter is Lisa.'

Then Marc talked about his career. He mentioned several personal financial details which his mother confirmed and he said he was worried about her.

'My mum shouldn't be working,' he said. 'I worked hard and made a lot of money, but I was ripped off. I thought a lot about my music but I was no good as a businessman.

'Fame and money came too quickly. I couldn't handle it. I wouldn't listen to my dad. I thought I was a big star but Dad always said "be careful".'

Phyllis nodded sadly. 'Yes, that's quite true. His dad did worry about him.'

And finally, like John Lennon, Marc's thoughts went back to his son. He was very proud of little Rolan.

'I was writing a song for Rolan just before it happened, you know,' he told me. 'A new song.'

Perhaps one day Rolan will write a song for his dad. Marc would like that.

# CHAPTER 5

It was Halloween night in America. All across the country excited children were scurrying from door to door shouting 'Trick or Treat!', adults dressed as witches and ghosts were hurrying to fancy dress parties and John and I, rather bemused by the eerie celebrations, were on our way to visit friends in Connecticut.

It was a cold night, the sort of night when the wind sighs in the trees, the dead leaves rustle in the gutter and normal objects cast strange, unnatural shadows. A night when even grown-ups hurry to switch on the lights.

Normally such things make me smile. I can understand the tingle of pleasant fear people enjoy listening to ghost stories or playing creepy games, but I can't share it. Ghosts, ghoulies and things that go bump in the night hold no terrors for me. If I see a ghost I simply wish him good day and ask how he is. But this particular Halloween I began to think the atmosphere was affecting me. The nearer we drew to the beautiful old mill house where our friends, the Wiehls, lived, the stranger I felt.

The car pulled into a lush shrub-lined drive, now a mass of heaving black shapes, and I began to feel distinctly weird. There was a hollow, drained sensation in my stomach that grew worse as we approached the house and by the time the car stopped I was feeling definitely ill.

I jumped out, thinking the fresh air would do me good, and then stopped dead. Whatever it was, I'd walked right into it. I was standing beneath a Victorian-style lamp-post from which swung a macabre Halloween pumpkin and the bad vibrations were all around. I wanted to scream and shout and throw things, but somehow I couldn't move.

'Why, Doris, what's the matter? Is something wrong?' It was Pam Wiehl, come to welcome us.

'Oh, no, no,' I stammered, forcing down the urge to scream. 'Let's go inside. I just feel a little, well, odd.'

It's such a beautiful place, I thought, glancing back at the lamp which glimmered on a breathtaking swimming pool. What on earth's going on?

Later, I found out. Pam's nineteen-year-old daughter, Sandy, had leapt up from the breakfast table one morning, rushed up to the roof and thrown herself off into the pool, which was empty at the time. Pam, hearing the crash, had raced outside and seen her daughter broken and dead at the bottom of the pool.

She told me later that she'd stood under the lamp, torn in two, paralysed with indecision. She didn't know whether to rush to her daughter or rush to phone an ambulance and, being pulled in two directions at once, she couldn't move at all. She stood there in agony, and when she opened her mouth to scream, no sound came out.

Strange as it may seem the sheer horror of that moment lived on. So powerful was the emotion Pam felt that morning, the air was still charged with it and any sensitive person would pick it up.

We had been meaning to visit the USA for a long time and our kind American friends pinned us down to autumn 1982. It's amazing how things snowball. On our last trip to New York we met a couple who'd lost their son, Greg, in a car crash. They came to me for a sitting and, as soon as I tuned in, four young people, all nineteen years of age, came bursting in to talk to us. One of them was Greg, and the others were called Sandy, Jamie and Chris.

74

They had all known each other on earth, they explained, and were still friends on the other side.

It turned out that the grieving but enterprising parents had formed themselves into a bereavement circle so that they could exchange help and comfort. Once Greg's parents had been to me for a sitting they were eager to persuade me to visit the rest of the circle and do the same for them.

'Next time you come to the States, come and stay with us and we'll introduce you to everyone,' they said. 'They'd be so pleased to meet you.'

I felt as if I knew Greg's family home already. During the sitting he had shown me a room which I took to be his parents' sitting-room. I saw a large window and on the wall beside it was a picture of Greg in casual clothes.

His parents, Pat and John, shook their heads blankly.

'No, that's not our living-room.'

'They don't recognize it, Greg,' I told him.

'Yes, they do.' He showed me the scene again but this time from further back so that I could see a red couch facing me. I described it to his parents.

'It's where you watch telly,' I added.

'Oh, our den!' they cried. 'Yes, it's exactly like that.'

Greg went on to talk of his passing. It was early morning just before dawn and a misty rain was falling. I had the impression of a wide open area, and a curve in the road, then a confusion of lights and a bang. Greg said he was killed instantly, his back and neck were broken and his chest was crushed. He was annoyed because his parents didn't receive all his belongings.

'They took my watch and I wanted Dad to have it. I'd just cashed my pay cheque but that was missing, too.'

'Yes, there was only one dollar in his wallet when we received it,' said Pat.

Most of all, Greg was sorry for the way he'd sometimes

75

treated his parents. 'I really socked it to them when I was growing up. But now I realize how much they loved me. Dad was disappointed because I didn't go to college, but I needed time to find myself. I think I was almost there, but then that stupid accident happened.'

Some weeks later, Greg's mother phoned to ask me yet again if John and I would be able to visit them. Within seconds of hearing Pat's voice, Greg was at my side.

'There's been a beautiful wedding,' he told me, 'and I went along. It was terrific!'

His mother gasped. 'Well, that's amazing,' she cried. 'Greg's sister, Debra, got married last week.'

'Did she marry Jean Marc?' I asked, remembering that during the original sitting Greg had mentioned Debra and a young man called Jean Marc. 'They're more than friends!' he told me.

'Why, yes,' said Pat. 'That's right, she did.'

This information made her more determined than ever that we should visit them.

'Sandy's parents are particularly anxious to meet you. After all, you did mention Sandy during the sitting.'

Well, of course, John and I would have loved to go but what with long-standing engagements and spells in hospital it was the end of 1982 before we could manage it. Yet once we arrived we were glad of our timing.

Connecticut in the fall was breathtaking. Never had we seen such colours. The air was crisp and sparkling and we drove down wide, open roads ablaze with fiery trees. Mile upon mile we saw nothing but brilliant trees each vying to outshine the one beside it. There were scarlets and coppers, acid yellows and lime greens, each one setting off the next until our eyes ached from gazing at them. John and I drove for miles without saying a word, so entranced were we with the scenery.

'What a pity you won't see it at its best,' people kept

saying to us and our jaws dropped. How could it possibly look lovelier than it did already?

'Why are the colours so much brighter than at home?' I asked John.

'Maybe it's the soil,' he suggested.

Whatever the reason, we were very thankful to have seen it.

As with all my trips abroad, word soon got round and television shows, public meetings and church services were added to my schedule. I ended up visiting New York and Baltimore as well as Connecticut but, unfortunately, on these tours the messages tend to blend into one another in my memory and afterwards I can only remember a few of the more striking ones.

I particularly remember the church service in Connecticut. Quite a few children came back to talk to their parents but after a while I kept hearing an insistent male voice. He wanted to talk to his wife.

I searched round the crowded hall looking for her and eventually I saw a light hovering around an intimidating, rather wealthy-looking lady. I could tell immediately that she didn't think much of this at all. In fact she told me later that she hadn't wanted to come and after what happened I can't say I blame her.

'I've got a message for that lady there,' I said, waving in her direction.

'Me!' cried the lady, aghast.

'Yes, I've got a man here and I think it's your husband.' The lady turned pale.

'Tell her to stop being so selfish,' said the crusty male voice. 'Tell her to stop hanging on to things.'

I passed this on as tactfully as I could. I do try to censor or at least modify certain messages especially in public where they could cause embarrassment. But on this occasion he wouldn't let up until he'd made his point.

'She's got two big houses,' he said, 'and now she's bought an apartment. What does she want three homes for at her age? She's hanging on to my clothes when she could give them away to be put to good use, and she's hanging on to me. Tell her to stop.'

This tirade quite took my breath away.

'He says you're hanging on to his clothes and you're hanging on to him,' I explained gently. 'He doesn't like it. He wants you to get rid of the things you don't need and start living.'

The woman looked as if she was going to choke. I must have frightened the life out of her, but fortunately her husband had said what he wanted to say and was willing to let other people take their turn so I was able to move on.

I was worried the lady might be offended, but once she'd had a chance to think about it I believe she felt calmer. She came up to see me afterwards.

'Well, I don't know what to say.'

'I'm afraid your husband was rather frank, dear,' I apologized, 'but he felt it was important you should understand these things.'

'Oh yes, it was typical of him,' she said.

Deep inside, I think it was a relief for her to be able to relax and let go at last. She was hanging on to her husband's things in a desperate attempt to hang on to her husband. Now she knew that she hadn't really lost him, that he was still close, she could relax.

In Baltimore it was a television show called *People Are Talking* that best stands out in my memory.

I was working with a combination of a live audience and unseen viewers who were telephoning the studio. There were two presenters, a man and a woman, and they seemed a bit uneasy with me. They didn't know what to expect and when the recipients of messages occasionally broke down in tears, overcome by emotion, they were rather alarmed.

I explained, as I usually do, that tears are a release and I'm very rarely asked to stop relaying the message, but the presenters were doubtful at first, although by the end of the show I think they'd changed their minds.

'Are you all right?' they kept asking members of the audience. 'Do you want her to stop?'

And time and time again they received the same answer. 'No, no, I'm crying because I'm happy.'

A few minutes into the show a young boy's voice came through. His name was Mitchell and he'd been killed in a motor-cycle accident.

'I went very quickly,' he said. 'My neck was broken.'

'Yes,' sobbed his mother who was in the middle of the audience. One of the presenters rushed over and put an arm round her shoulders but the woman didn't seem to notice.

'Mum said don't go,' Mitchell continued, 'but I went. I'm so sorry. It wouldn't have happened if I'd listened to her.'

'That's so true,' said his mother. 'He wouldn't listen to me. I didn't want him to go.'

But Mitchell didn't want her to be sad. He was an intelligent lad and he was determined to prove to his mother that he still spent a lot of time with her.

'She's been out with Betty,' he said.

'That's my friend,' his mother explained.

'And tell her I was with her when they went to the store and Mum bought a blouse. She paid for it and got as far as the door, then she said, "No, I don't think it's me," and she took it back again. That's typical of Mum. Always changing her mind!'

By this time, the mother's tears had dried up altogether

and her eyes were like saucers. She stared at me as if she suspected I'd been following her round the shop.

'That's exactly what happened,' she whispered.

The light moved on shortly after this and I was flitting from person to person when suddenly I got the name Jamie, followed by the name Griffin and the show came to a standstill. Nothing. Nobody could identify either of the names. There was complete silence.

Now I'll be the first to admit that I make mistakes and sometimes I mishear things, but these two names were quite distinct, not the confused blur you sometimes get when several voices are trying to communicate at once.

'Doesn't anyone know Jamie or Griffin?' I asked again.

Still nothing.

'They don't know you, dear,' I told the boy, but I was puzzled. It was so clear there must be a link with the programme somewhere. Perhaps the name was for one of the callers on the phone lines.

As it turned out I was right, except the person concerned hadn't even dialled the number at the time the message came through.

Unknown to me the mother of an eighteen-year-old boy named Jamie Griffin had been watching television when she suddenly heard me mention her son's name. Jamie had gone missing and the police suspected the worst, but Mrs Griffin refused to believe it. Her son was still alive, she was convinced. She believed he had probably lost his memory and was wandering around somewhere, confused and unaware of who he was.

When she heard me on the television she was seized with the idea that I might be able to tell her where she could find her son and she immediately phoned the police officer in charge of the case to ask if I would be allowed to help. The police had no objections, so they contacted the television station and, almost before I realized what

80

was happening, it was agreed that I would do a sitting before the cameras for Mr and Mrs Griffin.

As it turned out it was a very difficult project. As soon as the Griffins arrived I found that, like the police, I feared the worst. I kept hearing a young voice, a boy. I couldn't swear it was Jamie, and I wouldn't want to, because as I've said before I can make mistakes, but whoever it was I was getting details of a crime that had taken place.

The sitting started and immediately I was approaching a river bank. Then I stopped abruptly. I couldn't seem to move any farther. In my ear the name was being whispered but it sounded too implausible. I queried it but was given the same name again.

'The name of the river begins with a P,' I said, 'and it sounds like Powder River but that's ridiculous. There's also a waterfall nearby and that's called Powder Falls. I know it sounds ridiculous but that's what they say.'

'I think you must mean Gunpowder River and Gunpowder Falls,' said Mr Griffin.

Apparently the police thought these places figured in the case. Then I got the impression of a body which had been moved twice and I described a location. I was going up a narrow path in wild countryside.

'I've come to a place where the track forks and I can go right or left,' I told them. 'I'm going left and I can see an overhanging rock and a gorge below me.'

The parents shook their heads but Mrs Griffin looked alarmed.

'I don't care what anyone says, my son's alive,' she insisted. 'If you tell me different I won't believe it.'

The poor woman was obviously in a dreadful state.

'I can't tell you anything definite, dear,' I explained gently. 'All I can do is pass on what they tell me from the other side. Now, whoever it is I'm talking to, is giving me a name, a surname.' I mentioned it.

Again the parents looked blank, but I discovered afterwards that my information was correct. The officer in charge of the case phoned me later.

'That name you gave was my undercover name. No one apart from my chief and me know that name. Not even my wife.'

He went on to say that he, too, believed the body had been moved and they'd found a shallow grave in the location I'd described, but it was empty. He also knew the place where the path forked.

Mrs Griffin, by this time, had had enough. She must have known instinctively that there was no chance now of my telling her that her son was suffering from amnesia.

The person who was talking to me from the other side gave me the nickname of Jamie's grandfather and grandmother.

'A guess. A lucky guess,' said Mrs Griffin wildly.

He also mentioned Atlantic City.

'That's where my car was found,' said Mr Griffin. 'Jamie borrowed it to go to a Unity meeting at the church and he never came back. They found the car abandoned afterwards.'

Then came the name Michael.

'That's the boy who was with him,' said Mrs Griffin.

'They're telling me there was a row,' I explained. 'The boys were on their way to meet a man but there was a row.'

'Yes, but I kept telling you he's got amnesia,' hissed Mrs Griffin.

I stopped. It wasn't fair to continue. This lady had only called on me because she wanted me to prove her theory. She didn't want to know the truth. If I couldn't support her theory then she wouldn't listen. She wasn't ready yet to have an open mind and it wasn't right to force things on her that she wasn't ready to accept.

Of course, if the police found the body of her son, then that would be different. She would have to face brutal reality, but I could offer her no such tangible 'evidence' and it would be wrong to distress her unnecessarily. I thought back to the time years ago when John was missing, presumed dead after parachuting into Arnhem, and I was told by a medium that he was definitely in the spirit world. I had been devastated. What's more, the woman turned out to be wrong.

'I'm sorry, but the power's fading,' I said. 'I'm very tired. I think we'll have to call it a day.'

The cameras stopped, chatter broke out over the set, and people started walking about again. It was as if a spell had been broken.

Mr Griffin stared at me for a long time, then he came and sobbed on my shoulder. Mrs Griffin was quite composed. She patted her hair in case it had fallen out of shape, smoothed her clothes and stood up.

'My son is alive,' she told everyone who approached to offer her sympathy. 'I don't care what *anyone* says. I know he's alive.'

Of the two, I thought it was Mrs Griffin who was most in need of help.

I was all for leaving the case there but afterwards, when the officer in charge rang, he persuaded me to change my mind. I had come up with enough correct information to convince them that I might be of some practical use.

In particular, he was interested in the place I'd described where the path forked and a huge rock overhung the gorge.

'I know exactly where that is,' he said. 'If we took you to that spot, d'you think you might get any more information? We think it could be very important.'

83

'Well, I might,' I said. 'But I can't promise. Sometimes it works, sometimes it doesn't.'

In the end he convinced me I should try and we made arrangements to meet with the family and go together. But it wasn't to be. Somehow the press got to hear of the plan and contacted the police to see if they could go along as well. The police said no, but that didn't put them off.

'Doris, the police can't stop us. It's a free country, we can go where we like. But it's up to you. If you say you don't mind if we're there, they can't do anything about it.'

It was a terrible dilemma. If I said no, I suspected they'd write nasty things about me, but if I said yes, the police would be upset and so, very likely, would be the family.

I remembered the last time in New York when reporters had led me to believe that the family of a missing boy had agreed to media coverage of my investigations at the scene of the disappearance. The whole thing had turned into a circus and the mother, who it turned out had not been consulted, was almost hysterical. That had been a bitter lesson but I learned it well. I was determined it would never happen again.

What on earth could I do? The problem churned over and over in my mind. In the end it was John who came up with the obvious solution.

'Don't go,' he said. 'It's as simple as that. If you don't go, the press can't accuse you of being awkward and the parents can't accuse you of turning the case into a circus.'

So I didn't go. To those closely involved I explained the truth. To everyone else I had a bout of diplomatic ill health.

Yet, I still haven't finished with the case. The police were so convinced that I could help them, that they sent detailed maps of the area to my home in London so that I could work on them when I returned.

And I must say that one look at those maps was enough to make me very glad I didn't make the trip. The countryside is so very steep and rugged I reckon the journey would have finished me off!

As always, though, my most important work during that visit was the work I did in private. Amongst the pretty white clapboard houses of that north-eastern corner of America there was a lot of grief and tragedy and so many disturbed children. I couldn't understand why these children from beautiful homes with parents who clearly adored them were so mixed up. The ones who hadn't passed in tragic circumstances were receiving psychiatric help. What was the cause of all this confusion?

I asked Ramanov about it one night and he said he thought that the affluence was partly to blame. The parents worked terribly hard, some of them starting at half-past five in the morning and going on till late in the evening. The result was that they could afford a luxurious life-style but they expected their children to achieve the same success. Some children could cope with this but others couldn't and felt under pressure.

At the same time many parents seemed unusually protective of their children. One man kept telling me that he was trying to get his son to go back to school because it would be so much better for him. Yet that son was twenty-five years old, old enough to be a husband and father.

'When they are grown, you have to let children go,' said Ramanov. 'You have to let them be responsible for themselves because that is what they are here for. How else can they do the work they've been sent to do?'

We enjoyed our visit, but staying in the homes of bereaved parents was a heartrending experience. The children were so close that I kept bumping into them, and seeing them in their family setting brought home just how great a loss their parents had suffered.

In the home of Mark Ernst in New York, for instance, I went to the downstairs powder room and found Mark waiting for me in the corridor.

'Come down here and look at this, Doris,' he said and he led me through a door I hadn't noticed before, down another flight of steps to the basement.

'This is where a lot of my things were kept,' he explained, indicating the typical family jumble, 'but it got flooded one year.'

I'd first met Mark's parents months before when they came for a sitting at my flat in London. They were polite but rather wary of me at first and determined not to give anything away, so when they walked in I said:

'Oh, my dear, you've lost a child.' They denied it. I was convinced they had and that it was a son but, since they didn't want to mention it, I decided to let the sitting take its course and see what happened.

Mark's grandmother and great uncle and various other people came back, but eventually Mark wouldn't keep silent any longer.

He had been found dead in bed, he told me.

'Dad, forgive me,' he said. 'It wasn't me. I was killed. I didn't do it. Honest to God, I didn't do it.'

He was twenty-one and he was already over when they found him, he told me. But he was very concerned because people were saying he had committed suicide.

'They said I took an overdose, but I didn't,' he insisted. 'I was killed. I went to bed but to sleep.' There had been drink and medically prescribed drugs involved but Mark assured me that suicide wasn't in his mind. Unknowingly he had swallowed a combination that proved lethal. But it wasn't suicide. He loved his family and he wouldn't have wanted them to suffer.

'I know what they're doing,' he said. 'My brother Etan has got a new set of wheels. Tell him to be careful.'

'Has Etan got a new car?' I asked.

'No, a new motor-cycle,' said his father.

'Oh, that's what he means,' I laughed and explained what Mark had said.

By the end of the sitting the Ernsts were no longer wary.

'When you come to New York you must promise that you'll stay with us.' They insisted and we promised.

Well, of course, we took them at their word and we had a wonderful time. They looked after us as if we were VIPs. They had a beautiful house and we hadn't been there five minutes when Mark turned up.

One day I noticed his mother looking through a large folder and instantly Mark was at my side.

'That's mine,' he said. 'It's special.'

Sure enough, when I mentioned what he'd said, his mother opened the folder to show me a collection of Mark's old school essays that she'd treasured ever since he was a boy.

At poor Sandy Wiehl's home in Connecticut the vibrations were even stronger but, as I said before, it was in the garden by the pool that you could feel them most.

Her poor parents had been in a terrible state over the tragedy but when I did a sitting and spoke to Sandy I realized that, like Mark, she hadn't intended to kill herself.

She showed me what had happened and I had a swift impression of falling and suddenly halfway to the ground there came the thought: 'Oh no, there's no water in the pool.'

'I forgot the pool had been emptied,' Sandy told me.

It was a desperate gesture, intended to show how unhappy she was, but it had gone terribly wrong. The poor girl was ill, mentally ill.

'If I'd have been in my right mind I wouldn't have done it,' she explained. 'I had every opportunity but I went into depressions. One minute I was on top of the world, the next down on the floor in the flick of an eyelid.

'Nobody could do anything about it. And I was stupid, Doris. I did stupid things, things I knew I shouldn't be doing, just to be like all the other kids. But then afterwards I felt guilty and that made me more depressed. I was so mixed up.'

She was much better now, she said, and she wanted her mum and dad to know that she was very sorry for what had happened.

'What I did to my folks!' she sighed, lost for words to describe her behaviour. 'You see I thought I was grown up, but I wasn't really grown up at all. I must have been such a pain. I moped about the place and sometimes I lost my temper. I shouted at people. I understand now but at the time I was out of my mind.'

She gave her love to her family and talked a lot about Flip. I thought this must be some kind of fish but her parents roared with laughter.

'No, it's her brother Flip. A nickname for Philip.'

I had to laugh. 'I thought it was short for Flipper. I wondered if she had a pet dolphin or something!'

Flip apparently had seen Sandy since she passed but he thought he must have dreamed it. Sandy wanted him to know that it was real. She had also been around when her sister Kim, and Kim's friend Jenny May, had been discussing her in Kim's bedroom.

'They were trying on my clothes and talking about me and I shouted, "I'm here, damn you! I'm here!" but they couldn't hear me. It was so frustrating.'

Then she began speaking in French. She was quite fluent and I couldn't understand a word.

'I'm not showing off, Doris,' she said in English, after I was suitably baffled. 'I just wanted to show you what I was capable of and how much I might have achieved if I hadn't been ill.'

'Yes, she was very good at French,' her mother agreed.

Finally Sandy described a large wooden chopping board that stood on the worktop, or counter as the Wiehls called it, in the kitchen.

'One day I will knock on that board and then Mum will know I'm there,' she said. 'They're teaching me how to do it.'

I think Pam and John found this a little hard to believe but when we went into the kitchen I spotted the chopping board in exactly the position Sandy had described. Everything was quiet, however, and there was no sign of Sandy. It could take her years to learn how to knock, I supposed. I couldn't even guess how long such a skill would take to acquire.

But Sandy was obviously a fast learner. One day when we were gathered in the kitchen, but well away from the work top, we heard a loud rapping noise.

Pam opened the kitchen door. The hall was empty. She went to the window. There was no one there.

The knocking sounded again, hollow and insistent, and this time it came unmistakably from the chopping board.

'It's me,' cried Sandy. 'Have you forgotten?'

Pam looked at the chopping board in wonder. 'Well, I never would have thought it possible,' she murmured.

'You might as well get used to it,' I laughed. 'Now she's learned to do that, she'll be knocking all over the place, I expect.'

Quiet, beautiful Connecticut soon became the centre of a burst of activity – or at least that's the way it seemed to us. The bereavement circle was large and we visited home after home.

The Wiehls particularly wanted us to meet Dave and Skip Warren because their daughter, like Sandy, had taken her own life and there could be no doubt that she intended to. Betsy, who was twenty-one, worked in an animal clinic and one day she'd injected herself with a massive dose of animal poison, normally used to putting animals to sleep.

'You can't be right in the head to do a thing like that,' Betsy said when we started the sitting. 'It was a stupid thing to do but I'm happy now. I'm better off out of it.'

Her marriage had failed and she was very depressed.

'I couldn't seem to form relationships,' she said. 'I did try and I worked at it, but things always seemed to go wrong. I used to drink vodka, too. I started drinking in high school and it got worse and worse.'

She envied her sister Susanne because she had a baby, but these days she was mainly sorry about her mother. Skip had had several cancer operations and was coping very bravely, but Betsy felt that she hadn't offered her the support she should have done.

'I was so wrapped up in my own misery, Doris, I had no time for anyone else. If only I'd been kinder to my mother.'

Skip agreed that this was true. 'Yes, that's right. She had no time for my problems.'

Finally, Betsy was worried about her father.

'He feels guilty, Doris,' she said. 'When I started drinking he used to drink with me and now he blames himself. It wasn't his fault though. Please tell him to stop drinking so much. It's no answer.'

David had been pretty sceptical when the sitting started and, though he seemed impressed afterwards, I wasn't sure whether he would be affected by his daughter's words. But a couple of weeks later Skip rang me.

'And how's David?' I asked.

'Oh, he's being so good, Doris,' she said happily. 'He's cut down on his drinking and he's really trying. I'm so proud of him.'

As I said earlier, guilt is one of the emotions that haunts bereaved parents and it is quite extraordinary how they will go over and over the cause of death until they can find something to feel guilty about. It is no good outsiders getting impatient and accusing them of being ridiculous or of looking for something to make them unhappy. They can't help it and it seems to be a normal, if sad, reaction. I went through it myself when I lost John Michael and I've seen it in just about every bereaved parent I've ever met. It is cruel to tell them to 'pull themselves together'. They need understanding, love and gentle reassurance.

You wouldn't think, for example, that parents could blame themselves for their son's cancer, but the Kreegers did. They, too, were members of the bereavement circle. Their son, Scott, developed a cancerous mole at the age of twenty-one. It was a senseless tragedy for which no one was to blame. Yet Scott's mother blamed herself for giving him the wrong diet as a boy, and Scott's father blamed himself for passing on genes that were clearly faulty.

Scott, of course, blamed neither.

As soon as I walked in the room for the sitting I could tell that his father didn't hold with any of this nonsense, he'd only agreed to it to please his wife. Waves of disbelief and doubt were pouring out of him into the room, making it very difficult to concentrate.

Oh dear, I thought, we'll have to try and sort this out

first or we'll never get anywhere. 'Could you tell me something about him?' I asked the spirit world.

'He's an attorney,' came the reply.

I smiled at Mr Kreeger.

'Mr Kreeger, I know you don't think much of this sort of thing,' I told him. 'But I'm getting the message through that you're an attorney. Is that right?'

His face changed and I could see that he was shaken. 'Well, yes, yes, I am,' he floundered. 'But the Wiehls could have told you that.'

I didn't remember them doing so but he was right. They could have done.

Nevertheless the sceptical waves faltered and receded and I felt I'd be able to work more comfortably.

'Well, never mind,' I said. 'Let's see if we can find Scott and get him to convince you.'

I tuned in again and Scott didn't take much finding. He appeared in the room, between his parents, a very good-looking boy with striking colouring. Dark, almost black, hair, pale skin and deep blue eyes.

'What a handsome boy!' I couldn't help saying aloud.

'Yes,' sniffed his mother, 'he was.'

'No,' I corrected. 'He is.'

Scott sent his love to his parents, his sister Lisa and his girlfriend April. He had been very fond of April, he told me. He was a gentle artistic boy and he had been deeply involved in some sort of artistic project.

'Was it a hobby, love?' I asked him.

'No. It was my work.'

He tried to tell me what he did but I couldn't make head nor tail of it.

'I did it with Lisa,' he said. 'I did the designing and cutting out and we took it in turns to paint.'

Whatever could it be?

'Does this make sense to you?' I asked his parents.

'Oh yes,' they said. 'That's absolutely right.'

Well, that was the main thing. As long as they were happy it didn't matter if I didn't understand the evidence.

'There's a single red rose,' Scott continued.

At this his parents shook their heads. 'No, he didn't do any roses.'

'Well, did you give him a single red rose, when he was ill or at his funeral?' I suggested.

Again they shook their heads.

'Sorry, Scott,' I said. 'They can't place the rose.'

He was most insistent that the rose fitted in.

'Yes, but they can't accept it, love,' I explained. 'Maybe they'll think of it later.'

But Scott did not want to change the subject. He was absorbed by his work.

'Ask them to let you have a piece of my work as a memento of today.'

'Oh no, I couldn't do that.'

'Yes, you can,' he said. 'I want you to have something.'

'But I can't say that,' I protested. It would look as if I was taking advantage of his parents in the worst possible way.

'What can't you say, Doris?' asked Scott's mother.

'Well,' I hesitated. 'It seems a dreadful cheek, but . . .' and I told them what Scott had said. To my relief they didn't seem offended.

'What a good idea,' said Mrs Kreeger. 'We'd love you to have something to remember Scott by and what better keepsake than a piece of his work?'

'But what did he do?' I asked, wondering what I was letting myself in for. Supposing he carved life-size elephants or something?

Scott laughed at this.

'No, nothing like that, Doris,' he said and tried once again to explain but all I could hear was a 'sk, sk' sound.

Sketching perhaps? I wondered. But no. He wouldn't need to cut that out and paint it.

'It was scrimshaw,' said his mother. 'It's a dying craft. An old sailors' craft.'

Apparently, if I understand it correctly, patterns are cut into ivory, painted, and then sealed.

'Some of Scott's work has gone to the museum as an example of scrimshaw,' she continued, 'but there are quite a few pieces left.'

The sitting went on, with Scott giving names of various members of the family and family friends, then he talked about a holiday he'd enjoyed with his father.

'We went to New Zealand,' he said. 'We had a marvellous time, didn't we, pal?'

And at those words his father broke down and went and stood by the window, staring out over the garden. Apparently father and son had been very close and they always called each other 'pal'. That one little word had done more than anything else I'd said to convince Mr Kreeger that Scott was still near.

The sequel to this story came a few days later. Lisa brought it. I found a beautiful pendant on a red ribbon. The medallion was a piece of creamy ivory into which had been cut an exquisite red rose, every petal precise and perfect. Accompanying the gift was a note from the Kreegers.

'When we looked through Scott's things we came across this single red rose,' they wrote. 'This must have been the rose you were talking about and we're sure Scott would have wanted you to have it.'

I deliberated long and hard about what to do with that rose. If I wore it as a pendant it would only be seen on special occasions and would spend the rest of the time hidden away in my dressing-table drawer. Really, it deserved to be on permanent display.

In the end I made up my mind. Now it hangs beside the picture of Scott on my board of spirit children.

One of the nicest things that struck me about all these American children I spoke to was their thoughtfulness towards the people who were left behind, and this was demonstrated once again, just before I returned to England.

I was talking to Lisa Ernst, Mark's sister, on the telephone towards the end of our trip when Mark suddenly joined us.

'Ask her about Malcolm,' he said.

'Do you know anyone called Malcolm, Lisa?' I asked obediently.

'Oh, yes, he was a friend of Mark's,' she said. 'He's English, like you, but he's in hospital at the moment. They don't know what's wrong with him.'

Poor boy, I thought. It's bad enough to be in hospital at the best of times, but to be in hospital in a strange country thousands of miles from home, far from your family, must be awful.

'D'you think he'd like to hear another English voice?' I asked Lisa.

'Oh, I'm sure he would.'

I jotted down the number of the hospital and when I next had a spare moment I rang Malcolm. The boy was in a terrible state. Apparently he was suffering from some mystery virus, or so they thought, and he'd lost the use of his legs. He was lying there all alone with no family to visit him and the doctors didn't know what to do for the best.

At the sound of my voice he was so overcome he burst into tears.

'Oh, Doris,' he said. 'At a time like this the person you really want is your mother. But if I can't have my mother, you're the next best thing!'

We had a long talk, during which I told him about John's work as a healer.

'We're just about to go back to England,' I said, 'so I'm afraid John won't be able to do anything for you in hospital, but would you like him to put you on his absent healing list?'

John works with this list every night. He writes down the names and addresses of people who're sick, together with details of their ailments, and every night he sits down quietly and sends out healing thoughts to them.

'Well, it can't do any harm, can it?' said Malcolm. 'And the doctors don't seem to know what to do with me.'

So Malcolm went on the list.

A week later we were told he was on the mend, and the last we heard he was walking again and due to come out of hospital any day.

Whether it had anything to do with John I don't know. But I think we can safely say that Malcolm was given a helping hand from his friend on the other side.

# CHAPTER 6

How does that old saying go? Be it ever so humble, there's no place like home? Well, I must admit that after all my travels I've found it to be absolutely true. John and I had a wonderful time in America and we stayed in some magnificent houses with servants to wait on us and vast, manicured grounds.

Yet when we walked through the door of our little flat we both looked at each other and sighed with relief. Home! There was a pile of washing from our trip. Les and George had painted the flat right through and had the curtains cleaned. It was like a new flat. The view from the window was not of gently rolling lawns but the block of flats opposite. Yet it was our place and coming back to it was like swapping an elegant but tight dress for a battered old dressing-gown.

As always, our first priority was sleep. I can never sleep on planes and we'd been up all night on the flight back, but once the jet lag receded I was able to unpack and sort through my memories and mementoes of the trip.

There was a new pile of photographs for my spirit children board. I spread them out on the table in front of me. Scott, Greg, and Mark, Sandy and Betsy. I paused and put Sandy and Betsy side by side, studying their fresh young faces for signs of despair. But there was nothing to see. The torment that ruined their lives could not be captured by the camera.

'You can't be right in the head to do a thing like that,' Betsy had said.

'If I'd have been in my right mind I wouldn't have done it,' Sandy had cried.

Two poor sick girls, whose sickness couldn't be seen and therefore couldn't be understood by ordinary people.

I think there is probably much more mental illness around, unrecognized and untreated, than people realize. I wonder why it is that we can accept the fact that a body will fall ill with colds, flu or worse, quite frequently through a lifetime, but we can't accept that a mind could suffer similarly.

Perhaps people like little Paul, the boy who took his clothes off when he was being ignored, are the lucky ones. Paul was mentally retarded and it was fairly obvious, so people could see and understand his condition and they treated him sympathetically. No one expected too much from Paul, and when he achieved something they were pleasantly surprised. Paul never felt a failure and his parents, Jean and Steve, adored him.

At the sitting, Paul's grandpa, Joseph, spoke first.

'Paul couldn't talk on earth because he had a convulsion when he was a baby,' Joseph told me. 'And Jean and Steve are worried because he was unconscious when he passed and they couldn't say goodbye.'

I passed this on and Jean and Paul agreed that it was true.

'Well, you mustn't worry about it,' I assured them. 'Because Paul didn't know anything about it and there was no need to say goodbye. He hasn't gone. He's with you still.'

Paul was grinning away while I said this and to prove I was right he piped up:

'Yes, and Sarah's got the pennies out of my money box.'

'Yes!' cried Jean. 'Sarah's Paul's sister. That's the only thing she asked for. Two or three days after he died she said, "Paul won't need his pocket money now, Mum, so can I have it?" '

'She's got my teddy in bed with her, too,' Paul added.

Jean and Steve exchanged looks. This too was true and an expression of joy began to spread across Jean's face. But Paul was still chattering away. On the other side he had found his voice and he liked using it. He said his daddy had put a rose in a vase beside his photograph and he liked that. He thought the month of February was important.

'Yes,' said Jean. 'He died on the fourteenth and it would have been his fifth birthday on the twenty-fourth.'

But Paul was off again. 'Look at this. It's our house.' Suddenly I was walking through a front door and upstairs. 'See there's a new stair carpet,' he said as we climbed and when we got to the top we turned right and went into the bathroom. I was confronted by mirrors.

'This is the best room,' said Paul.

Quickly I explained where I was to his mummy and daddy.

'As I got into the bathroom there are mirrors facing me,' I explained.

'That's right,' said Jean. 'The whole wall's covered in mirror tiles.'

'Well, one day,' I told her, 'you will walk in there and see Paul's face reflected in the mirrors facing the door. You'll just see his face smiling at you. Don't be afraid when it happens. Just say "Hello son" and talk to him.'

Jean and Steve looked pretty amazed at this information but Paul seemed so sure he would do this one day, probably with his grandpa's help, that I had to mention it and I'm convinced that sooner or later it will happen. It must have been pretty hard for his parents to swallow at that time, however, but Jean did agree that the bathroom was special to Paul.

'He spent every night of his life in that bathroom,' she explained. 'He loved a bath and he loved to watch himself splashing about, in the mirrors. It was one of his favourite games. We all used to enjoy it because it made Paul so happy.'

'I liked going out in the car, too,' Paul interrupted. 'It was a new car and I used to look at everything out of the windows.'

'Yes, he did,' said Jean, then she turned to her husband. 'You see, I told you he knew we'd got a new car. He was much brighter than people thought. I was sure he could tell the difference between the new car and our old one.'

The sitting went on, more relatives came back to have a word with the young couple and that was when, my attention being diverted from him, Paul stripped off his clothes.

As it turned out, it was the best thing he could have done. Steve had been sitting there listening to what was going on with an incredulous expression on his face. He had come to the sitting sceptical, what he had heard had amazed him, but he still couldn't quite believe – until Paul took off his clothes in a gesture both typical and unique. There was no way I could have guessed such an unusual habit.

After the sitting, Jean and Steve lingered to talk to me about their son. He was such a happy boy, they explained, and they missed him so badly. It didn't matter a scrap to them that he was retarded. They loved him as much as it is possible to love a child. Any ill-informed person who said that they were better off without him was cruelly mistaken. Paul might have been damaged but he had his own special part to play in the family.

A few days later they wrote to me, thanking me for the sitting and with the letter was a tiny brooch in the shape of a butterfly.

'Please wear this brooch in memory of Paul,' Jean wrote. 'We think of him as our little butterfly.'

As I read the letter tears came into my eyes. What a

perfect description of their little boy. Vivid and beautiful, brightening everything he touched and then gone in a flash – just like a butterfly.

There was no question that Paul was a wanted child and Jean and Steve coped well, but other parents aren't so lucky. Some children are so badly handicapped that, although their parents love them, they can't care for them at home. Sadly, there are also other children whose parents reject them almost at birth for the same reason. Yet, in a way, there is no need to be too sorry for these little ones because often they are quite happy in their own little worlds.

You hear a lot of horror stories about the things that go on in mental hospitals. I couldn't say whether or not they are true, all I do know is that when I spent some time working in a mental hospital after I finally qualified as a nurse in my forties, I saw only love, devotion and extraordinary patience.

I'm not saying that the nurses were all saints; far from it. It was just that those kids, no matter how damaged, were so wonderful in their own special ways, that you couldn't help loving them.

To be frank, there were some really horrifying cases in the hospital. Or at least they were horrifying at first sight. But it was amazing how quickly you got used to them.

I remember the day, not long after I'd started work at the hospital, that I was sent down to help out at the new infirmary. They were short of staff and, despite my inexperience, they thought I might be useful.

The sister was standing beside a cot as I walked in and she was holding a baby in her arms.

I hurried over to her in that brisk nurse's walk that I'd recently acquired. Fast and efficient but with no suggestion of panic.

'Hello, my name is Nurse Stokes,' I said. 'I've been sent down to help you out, Sister.'

She glanced up at me and her eyes held mine for a moment or two as she silently weighed me up. Then she smiled.

'Oh good. Well here, hold this. This is Nigel.' She handed me the baby.

By this time everyone knows how I feel about babies and I took the little scrap with pleasure. I should have noticed and been warned that something was wrong by the way Sister didn't move off after passing the boy to me but remained where she was, watching my face. But I wasn't warned. I hardly even registered it.

I was instantly enthralled, the way I always am when I've got a baby in my arms, and I looked down at little Nigel. The most beautiful little face looked back at me and a pair of baby blue eyes stared into mine. My face was folding instinctively into a smile, when I noticed something with a cloth over it next to Nigel's head.

Curiously, I lifted the cloth, and my stomach seemed to fall away. There was another head underneath, with little indentations where the features should have been.

Nigel was one of nature's mistakes.

I bit my lip hard, so as not to pass out and, as the room swung back into focus, I glanced up at Sister. She was watching me gravely.

I took a deep breath.

'What a dear little face,' I said as calmly as I could.

Sister smiled. 'Yes, isn't it? Right, carry on then, nurse,' and she bustled away obviously satisfied that I could cope.

There were more horrors in store. Later that morning one of the other nurses came over.

'You're the new nurse, aren't you?' she said quickly.

'Well, you'll be going in to see the new baby. Take a grip of yourself. I nearly fainted when I went in.'

Before I could question her she was gone. Uneasily, I finished mixing the feed I was preparing. What on earth could be worse than poor Nigel?

I didn't have long to find out.

'Ah, Nurse Stokes,' said Sister, coming alongside me suddenly. 'Leave that for a moment, would you. You'd better come and see the new baby.

This time I was prepared. Grimly, I followed her up the ward to a special room where a single cot stood alone. I steeled myself firmly as I approached it. The warning was a great help and this time I had no fear of fainting, although the poor little mite was a dreadful sight.

She was premature, she had spina bifida and something else had clearly gone wrong, because her head went up into a sharp point and she seemed to have no flesh on her bones. The skin hung in folds from her pathetic, wasted limbs.

I swallowed hard but I had a good grip on myself as I'd been advised.

Nevertheless, I think I went home that night in a state of shock. It seemed so cruel that those poor misshapen children should have been born. Wouldn't it have been better for them to pass over at birth then linger in this way?

I couldn't understand it. I still don't understand it, although now I know there must be a reason and that those innocents must have a part to play, no matter how obscure it seems to us. All I can say with certainty is that they are not unloved and I believe they are not unhappy.

Within days I found I didn't notice Nigel's deformity. I didn't even see it. When I looked at him all I saw was that lovely face. To me he was a beautiful baby.

It was the same with the new baby in the special room.

Before the week was over us nurses were falling out about whose voice she recognized and who she liked best. Of course, looking back I don't suppose she recognized any of us, but we liked to think she did.

Some of the sick children on the ward did know us. There was Geraldine who'd been in a car crash. She wasn't marked at all but she couldn't see and she couldn't sit up. Yet she was a cheerful little thing and she knew your voice.

Every morning I used to tickle her and say 'Who's a pretty girl then, Geraldine?' And she'd gurgle away with pleasure.

Then there was Anthony. He was about four or five but he had water on the brain which left him with a great swollen head and a tiny undersized body. Nevertheless, he knew when he was wet or cold or hungry and when you talked to him he'd smile up at you.

You soon got to love them, those poor little children and, despite everything, the ward was a happy place.

Not all the children were as severely handicapped as Nigel, Geraldine and Anthony. Often they were capable of far more than anyone believed possible. That's what made working with them so rewarding.

You weren't supposed to have favourites but you couldn't help it and one of mine was a spastic girl called Patsy Kelly. She couldn't walk and she had to have her hands tied up in an apron because for some reason she kept putting them down her throat and making herself sick. Despite this, she was a lovable character.

'Who's a bad 'un?' I used to pretend to scold. 'I'll give it to you. Who's a bad 'un?' and she used to rock herself in delight and laugh till the tears rolled down her cheeks. She may not have known what the words meant but she recognized them and understood that they were spoken with love.

One day we were getting the children ready for a walk in the gardens. It was quite a laborious procedure because they all had to be taken to the lavatory before going out. We used to round them up and change them one by one and sit them in the corridor to wait until everyone was ready.

This particular morning I thought I'd finished when I discovered that little Sharon had had another mishap and her knickers were soaking wet.

I whisked her up, took her back and laid her on the changing table again.

'Who's a bad 'un!' I was saying to her as I worked. 'I'll give it to you! You wet these knickers and I'll have your guts for garters!'

Sharon thought this was a tremendous joke. She was giggling and I was laughing and I suppose my voice must have been louder than I realized because outside in the corridor, Patsy Kelly, who couldn't walk, suddenly got to her feet and, beaming all over her face and rocking like a boat, she tottered towards the door from which she could hear those familiar words.

'Who's a bad 'un!'

The incredible event was the talk of the hospital for weeks and Sister never got over it. Such things didn't happen after all . . .

One day Sharon, as well, shook me rigid. She was a pretty girl of five with brown curly hair and blue eyes. She had been in the hospital all her life. We were the only family she'd ever known. She had never spoken and we all assumed she couldn't.

Then came the time when she caught German measles along with several other children. This was serious, as it could lead to an epidemic in the hospital from which some of the patients might not recover. Great precautions were taken which involved a lot of extra work for the nurses.

Sheets were wrung out in carbolic and hung in lines across the ward. The doorknobs were covered in carbolic and the nurses had to wear rubber gloves.

Inside the isolation area the children just lay in their beds with nothing to do. I felt sorry for them. It seemed boring to me to have to lie there all day so, when I was on duty, I used to sing to them to liven things up.

I'm absolutely tone deaf and not by any stretch of the imagination a singer, but nevertheless I enjoy singing and those children, who after all knew no better, seemed to enjoy listening to me. I used to go from cot to cot singing each child a different song and for some reason I chose a jolly little tune called *He Wore a Tulip*, for Sharon.

'He wore a tulip, a bright yellow tulip and she wore a red red rose,' I used to sing and her eyes would widen and she'd listen to this with rapt attention. After a few days she began coming to the end of her cot when I started to sing and she'd pull herself up and look right into my eyes and if I stopped singing she rubbed my face until I started again.

She never tired of this game and for me it became a routine. Then one day I started off in the same old way:

'He wore a tulip, a bright yellow tulip and she wore a . . .'

'Wed wed wose,' interrupted a strange little voice.

I stopped dead and stared at Sharon. Surely that wasn't her? She couldn't speak.

'He wore a tulip,' I began again cautiously. I was probably imagining things but I might as well put it to the test. 'A bright yellow tulip and she wore a . . .' I paused.

'Wed, wed wose,' Sharon finished.

If the bottle of baby lotion in my pocket had suddenly offered an opinion on the weather I couldn't have been more surprised.

'There's a clever girl, Sharon!' I cried and I tried it

again. Each time I sang the song, Sharon finished it for me.

'Sister, come and listen to this,' I called when her head appeared round the carbolic sheet. 'Sharon's just spoken.'

'No!' said Sister, coming over to the cot. 'She's never spoken in five years.'

'Well, listen.' I launched into another rendering of *He Wore a Tulip*. At the appropriate place I waited and, sure enough, in chimed Sharon:

'Wed wed wose . . .'

That song became Sharon's party piece. She had never spoken, and she never did speak, but you sing *He Wore a Tulip* and she always came in at the end.

It wasn't just the nurses who found the children surprising, sometimes they amazed their parents as well. There were some parents who never visited, some who came every week, and some who could only get to the hospital every now and then.

It was the irregular visitors who got the most surprises. I remember one little girl called Sylvia who was in a shocking state when she was brought to us. I don't know what happened to her mother, but her father had to go away to work and he'd left Sylvia in the care of an elderly relative who could hardly look after herself let alone a backward child as well.

By the time the social workers heard about Sylvia she was a mess. I'll never forget the day they brought her in. I'd never seen a child in such a state.

She was filthy, her hair was so matted and unwashed it looked like an ancient dog blanket, and she was thin and under-nourished. We could only guess at her former life-style from her behaviour with us.

The first thing to do with her was to give her a bath, but she was obviously a complete stranger to washing. She was terrified of water. She screamed and kicked and yelled and it took two of us to get her in the bath and even then she wouldn't sit down. We had to wash her standing up.

Finally after a good half hour's struggle, a thin, bedraggled little creature emerged from the bathroom, rather sorry for itself and resembling a drowned rat, but clean.

'Come on, love,' I said taking her hand. 'Let's get you something to eat.' That was when we discovered more about her former life. Faced with the meal table Sylvia was totally at a loss. She'd never sat at a table before and she'd never eaten proper food or, if she had, it was so long ago she couldn't remember it. The old lady had existed on bread soaked in sweet tea and so had Sylvia.

In those first few weeks life with Sylvia was hard work. She had been happy enough with the old lady and she couldn't understand why she should change. But gradually she settled down and, as a proper diet, regular washing and plenty of sleep began to take effect, we realized that she was a very beautiful child.

Her hair, which had been lank and lacklustre, grew thick and glossily black, her skin which had been pale and delicate turned creamy pink with health and suddenly you noticed that her eyes were enormous and the deepest shade of blue I'd ever seen.

The months passed and then came the news that Sylvia's father was coming to visit her. I'd grown very fond of Sylvia by this time and I wanted her to make a good impression so I went to the store and found her a pretty blue dress the colour of her eyes. Then on the great day I rushed down to the city before going on duty and bought a length of blue ribbon to match the dress.

Back at the hospital I brushed Sylvia's hair until you could practically see your face in it, dressed her in the

God's Special Children

Paul — he loved to watch himself splashing about in the mirrors

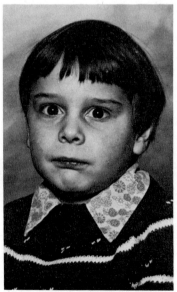

Steven and Helen, beautiful children

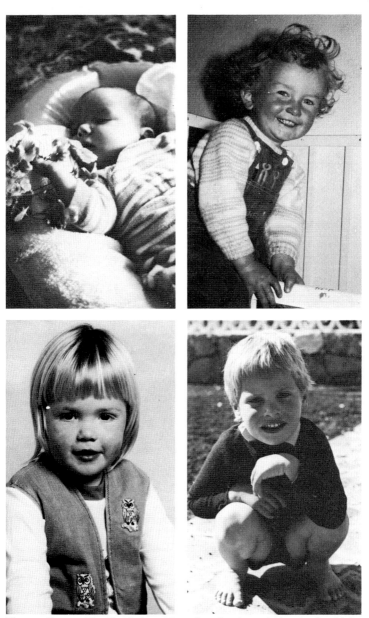

Thomas, Duncan, Tennille-Marie and Peter from Sweden — 'old souls who didn't need much time on earth'

Betsy: 'I'm better off now'

Sandy from Connecticut, only 19

Shirley — she was so beautiful, but she's happier now

Morag & Gail — such sadness

Nigel at 2 with his sister, Susan

Marc Bolan — he was gentle and kind-hearted

Glen: 'I spend a lot of time in the halls of music'

Mark from New York, fatal pills

Richard Beckinsale, star of *Rising Damp* and *Porridge* — 'a very sensitive person'

new dress and tied the ribbon into a bow. She looked wonderful.

'Who's a beauty then?' I said taking a step back to admire her. 'Don't you look nice? Good enough to eat.' She dimpled with pleasure.

Hand in hand we went downstairs and I tapped on the nursing officer's door.

'I've got Sylvia here for visiting,' I said, putting my head round the door.

'Right. I'll be there in a minute, nurse,' said the nursing officer, collecting up the papers on her desk and, thinking she meant she'd be following us, I walked on with Sylvia to the visitors' room.

There was a man standing in the hall as we passed but I didn't give him a second glance. I assumed he had an appointment with someone.

Anyway, when we reached the visitors' room it was empty. Oh no, I thought, don't say he's not going to come. But I didn't want Sylvia to sense my disappointment so I sat her on my knee and started telling her a story.

A few moments later we heard voices in the hall.

'Where's Sylvia?' asked the nursing officer in surprise.

'I don't know,' answered an unknown male voice. 'I haven't seen her.'

'But Nurse Stokes has only just brought her down,' said the nursing officer with a hint of impatience creeping into her voice. 'Didn't she take her into the visitors' room?'

As she spoke, we could hear footsteps crossing the hall, the door opened, and the nursing officer and the man we'd passed in the corridor appeared in the doorway.

'Why, yes. Here she is,' said the nursing officer.

The man's mouth just fell open as he took in his daughter. She looked so beautiful he hadn't recognized her.

The sequel to that story is that Sylvia turned out to be a talented artist. Years after I left the hospital she sent me a beautiful picture which I still treasure and to this day she paints the most fantastic oil paintings.

It is amazing how much the children do remember. There was a blind girl called Geraldine, for instance, who came to us when she was very small. At first, she was a bright little thing who chattered away and helped us look after the tots. The only problem with her was that she kept hitting herself in the eyes. Whether it was in frustration because she couldn't see, we didn't know, but to prevent her harming herself she had to have her hands fastened behind her back all the time.

It used to break my heart to see her like that and I used to think, poor little girl your arms must ache. So when I undressed her ready for bed I used to untie her arms and stretch them over her head and to the sides. To distract her from hitting her eyes during these exercise sessions I used to say to her:

'Tomorrow I'm going to bring you a parcel and what will be in it?'

Geraldine would say, 'An apple!'

I'd say, 'And an . . .'

'Orange!'

'And a piece of . . .'

'Chocolate cake!' Geraldine would cry.

She began to look forward to our parcel sessions at bedtime and all the time she was making good progress. Eventually she was judged to have improved so much she was allowed home.

We never did find out what happened or what went wrong but somehow Geraldine deteriorated and she was sent back to us. She never spoke again.

The years went by, I left the hospital and long afterwards I went back for a visit. As I walked through the grounds I noticed a group of patients sitting in a circle on the grass and a scattering of the nursery children skipping round them.

The children spotted me first and came running up shouting, 'Nurse Stokes! Nurse Stokes!'

I was busy saying, 'Hello, love, hello, love,' to each one individually when suddenly I heard one of the adult patients say:

'Would you look at her!'

I glanced up to see Geraldine, in the adult wing now, coming towards me. She was blind, but her sense of hearing was so acute she knew exactly where I was. She came straight over, put her head on my chest and started to cry. And I thought, they do remember, they do.

Afterwards I made my way from the gardens into the hospital and arrived at one of my old wards just on bath time to see one of my other favourites, Jenny Lee.

'Hello, Jenny,' I said going up to her.

'Hello,' said Jenny impassively as if she'd never seen me before in her life.

'I've brought you a pat of chocolate!' I whispered.

She beamed all over her face and took it eagerly.

'You took me to the pictures, didn't you, Nurse Stokes?' she said as plain and distinct as anything, 'to see my sister.'

I was amazed. It must have been three years ago or more since I'd taken her to the hospital cinema to see her sister, Frances Lee, in a film. Yet, despite the fact that I wasn't in uniform and she didn't know I was coming, Jenny remembered both me and the occasion.

Sometimes, of course, it was heartbreaking. We knew that many of the children had short life expectancies but knowing that didn't make you stop loving them and didn't make it any easier when they passed. Although I wasn't working as a medium while I was nursing I couldn't switch off my psychic powers, and therefore I always knew when a child didn't have long to go. Yet knowing in advance was probably harder to face than not knowing, because I felt so helpless.

When Patsy Kelly's time was close I was frustrated to find that I'd been sent to work on a different ward, the adult ward, so I had hardly any time to be with Patsy. That was probably why I was transferred. Yet it's amazing what can happen.

One afternoon I was asked to take a message to the sister of the nursery ward, whose office happened to be close to the room where Patsy lay unconscious with a nurse at her side twenty-four hours a day.

I obediently delivered the message but afterwards, instead of going straight back to my work, I couldn't resist looking in to see how Patsy was.

To my surprise the nurse on duty seemed to be expecting me. 'Stokes, an amazing thing just happened!' she said excitedly. 'When you were talking to Sister just now I'll swear Patsy could hear your voice. She's been unconscious all this time yet as soon as you started talking she opened her eyes, grinned all over her face and tried to sit up.'

I looked down at Patsy, now as silent and unmoving as she had been the last time I peeped in, and it seemed very hard to believe.

'Hello, Patsy,' I whispered. 'How's my bad 'un then?' There wasn't a flicker and in the distance I could hear the murmur of spirit voices come to take her home. My eyes filled with tears.

'It won't be long now, nurse,' I said, my voice wobbling and I turned and hurried away. It wouldn't do to be caught sobbing on duty.

A few hours later Patsy passed over. She was fourteen years old.

Later I went to visit her in the chapel and when I saw how lovely she looked I knew that it was selfish of me to wish her back. I would miss her infectious laughter on the ward but she was happier now with her relatives on the other side.

'Well, you're at peace now, Patsy,' I said aloud as I left her for the last time.

But, unlikely as it might sound, there was more fun and laughter than tears. After tea when I was on duty I organized hilarious games of hokey-cokey in the ward and during the day when the weather was fine, we played 'Here We Come Gathering Nuts in May' on the field outside.

The children varied enormously in intelligence but this didn't cause any problems. We put the brightest next to the most handicapped and they helped each other. It was wonderful to see how patient the children were with each other and how they looked after the least able. A child who was blind need never fear the teasing you might expect from normal playmates. There was always someone there to see they came to no harm.

Some of the children, particularly the epileptics, were extremely intelligent. We used to keep a record of the number of fits each child suffered and if they went for two years without a fit we used to have a party.

They took great interest in the recording of fits and they knew how long they had to go before their party. Those who achieved the two years were ecstatic. They came rushing into the ward, their faces alight with pleasure, shouting:

'I'm out of the fit book, nurse. I'm out of the fit book.'

Others were so clever you wondered why they were in the hospital at all. One woman had been there as long as anyone could remember, so long, in fact, that I couldn't find anyone who knew why she'd been admitted in the first place.

Perhaps years ago she'd had an illegitimate baby at a time when women who got into trouble were sometimes hidden away so as not to bring shame on the family. Anyway, whatever the reason, this woman was so settled in the hospital she wanted no other way of life and it would have been cruel to push her into the outside world.

She was happy and she ran the private ward. It was unofficial, of course, but she knew how it worked far better than any of the nurses and whenever a new nurse arrived she would take her under her wing and show her how everything was done.

Other patients weren't so obviously intelligent but they were very talented in other ways. I've still got an exquisite work basket made for me by one of the patients and there were two girls who could knit beautifully. No matter how intricate the pattern it presented no problems to them. It reached the stage where if any of us nurses got into a muddle with our knitting we'd take it to them. They could look at it, spot what was wrong, pull it apart and put it right, in minutes.

Of course there were plenty of other patients who gave no trouble but who were harmlessly eccentric. One of them was a little girl called Emily. Emily was a sweet, gentle girl who had an obsession with hats and handbags. She was devoted to her collection and I used to beg all the hats and handbags I could get hold of to help her increase it. Emily gave offence to no one and she said very little. All she wanted to do was put a hat on her head, a handbag over her arm, and walk up and down the corridor. After about ten minutes she's go back to the ward, change her hat and handbag and repeat the process.

She would cheerfully play this solitary game all day long and nobody could persuade her to do anything else.

Emily's obsession was unusually deep, but all the children, even the most handicapped, were very attached to their few possessions. They all had to have something that was theirs, even if it was only a carrier bag with a postcard in it. They would take these possessions everywhere with them, even to bed.

Entertaining people with such mixed abilities could have been difficult, but the hospital had an enlightened attitude. Facilities were provided and the patients benefited from them in different ways, according to their capabilities.

On Good Friday, for instance, there was a religious service followed by a film about the crucifixion. Some patients enjoyed it in the normal way, others had no idea what was going on but liked to hear the singing and watch the moving pictures.

The vicar had to be ready for anything. One year the religious service seemed to be dragging on longer than usual and the children were shuffling a bit, wondering when the film was going to start.

Unfortunately the vicar didn't seem to be aware of the restlessness of his flock and he launched into another lengthy prayer. He didn't get far. Two lines into the prayer a little boy near the front of the hall piped up:

'Oh bloody 'ell, our men!'

There was a stunned silence. Then the vicar said, very quickly:

'In the name of the Father, the Son and the Holy Ghost, Amen,' missing out the whole of the middle section of the prayer and brought the service to a swift end.

There was no point in scolding the boy. He didn't understand what it was all about. All he knew was that when he said 'Our men' the picture would start.

There were quite a few mongols at the hospital and

they were delightful, so cheerful and affectionate. They used to wash our cups out for us and rub our feet after a long day on the ward. They loved music and had regular dancing lessons. Once a month the older ones had a proper dance with a band from outside.

This was the highlight of their days. The girls used to make long evening dresses to wear and the nurses would make up their faces for them. They thought it was marvellous. Out on the dance floor they'd bow and curtsey to each other and then swing round the room beaming at the nurses as they sailed past as if to say, 'Look at us!'

There were usually few nurses in attendance but we took part in the fun and, if we were asked to dance, we danced. The boys would have been very offended if we refused.

Many of these older ones were allowed out into the town on their own and, like small children, they were innocently determined to enjoy themselves and were quite uninhibited.

Often John and I would be quietly shopping in a crowded store when suddenly a great yell would ring out, startling shoppers.

'Yoohoo! Yoohoo! Nurse Stokes! Mr Stokes! Yoohoo!'

Heads would turn and John and I would look up to find we were being greeted from the other side of the store by a merry bunch of waving patients who were quite unaware of the disturbance they were causing.

These patients became highly independent and this was encouraged. A large house was bought for them just up the road from the hospital and the rooms were beautifully fitted out, two beds to a room, with matching bedspreads and curtains and good quality carpets on the floor.

There was one nurse and a sister on duty but the patients more or less took care of themselves. In the early days the staff used to walk them backwards and forwards to the main hospital for school or classes or to work in the laundry, but after a while they put in a petition asking for the right to make the journey unaccompanied.

They went down to the town without an escort, they said, so why couldn't they be trusted to go to the hospital on their own?

Initiative was rewarded and they got their permission.

In the evenings they ran their own club and this was an entirely private affair. Strictly no admittance to nurses without an invitation. It was all very innocent. They spent the evenings concocting weird meals and dancing to the music on the radio. John and I were invited one evening and they cooked us a feast of bacon and onions. It arrived swimming in grease but we had to eat it. We wouldn't have hurt their feelings for the world.

They all stood round, bursting with pride as they watched us eat, saying:

'Isn't it good? Isn't it good?'

And, smiling through the grease, we assured them it was delicious.

I don't want to give the impression that working with the mentally handicapped is all joy and fun, because it isn't. It's exhausting, demanding and very hard work. There are difficult patients and some can turn violent. I should know because I had to give up nursing after being injured by one. But I would like to stress that in my experience mental hospitals are not all gloom and misery.

Of course, patients have their off days. Don't we all? But most of the people I worked with were content and secure, happy to stay in a protected work where no one expected more from them than they were capable of achieving.

# CHAPTER 7

'Oh, eh, hello Doris. I hope you don't mind. I've brought my friend with me.' There is a slight pinkening of the cheeks and the eyes fall to study my shoes. 'Well, you see I was a bit scared to come on my own.'

This is the nervous sitter. I know her well.

'That's all right, love. I don't mind a bit,' I say. 'Come on in.' And I take her inside, knowing that after a few minutes she'll be quite relaxed.

It's amazing how many people are frightened when they arrive for their first sitting. They think I'm going to fall into some terrifying trance, or draw the curtains and condemn them to darkness and supernatural shadows.

In fact, we merely settle ourselves into armchairs and have a chat, in broad daylight unless, of course, it's winter when I might have to turn on the electric light.

Afterwards the sitters unanimously agree that there is nothing remotely scarey about the process. Yet people who have never experienced it still frequently ask:

'But what *happens* at a sitting?'

So for all those who are still curious I thought it might be interesting to record a sitting in full, as it happened.

Below is a transcript of a sitting I did with Susan Otter and her husband in early 1982, omitting only some personal details that are private to the couple and some irrelevant conversation.

DORIS: I think by the size of his light that Simon hasn't been over a year yet, has he?
SUSAN: March.

DORIS: Now he's talking about someone called Bill. Do you know a Bill?

SUSAN: No.

DORIS: That's funny. I thought he said Bill. It can't be right then. It's not Bert, is it?

SUSAN: Yes, that's my father.

DORIS: That's it. He said you'd been talking to someone about him but I thought he said Bill. Oh, he's saying 'No I didn't, I said Bert. I speak English, don't I?' He's a cheeky young thing.

SUSAN: Yes, he was.

DORIS: Now he says there's been a birthday since he went over.

SUSAN: Yes, in May. He would have been nine.

DORIS: He said they all cried and I had some flowers and me Grandad Bert said why couldn't it have been me?

SUSAN: Yes, he did say that.

DORIS: He says: but I'm all right, Mummy. It was very quick. He went out and never came home.

SUSAN: No.

DORIS: And I never saw me daddy. I saw him the night before.

SUSAN: Yes.

DORIS: I feel as if I was thrown. As if something hit him very quickly and he was falling into unconsciousness.

SUSAN: Yes, the disease hit him very quickly.

DORIS: And he never came round again. The back of his head hurt.

SUSAN: It did. It was a brain disease.

DORIS: That's the only indication he can give me. Call me Granny Doris, love, all the other kids do. I've got two grannies already, he's saying. Well, I'm an extra one, darling. But he said it happened within twenty-four hours, love. Incredible. From being a

119

healthy little boy he got very hot and he felt sick and I fell asleep then.

SUSAN: Yes.

DORIS: He said you took a sweater out and you kissed it and put it back. Didn't you, love?

SUSAN: Yes, I did.

DORIS: You see, he was there then when you did that and he saw you. He hasn't gone away. He's round the house still.

SUSAN: Yes, I know, I can feel it.

DORIS: Now, who's Philip he's talking about.

SUSAN: That's his dad.

DORIS: That's what I've been waiting for. I said to him, I know he's your daddy but what's his name?

DORIS: Right, so that's your daddy. Now, are you going to let anyone else speak? No, no he's not going to let anyone else talk . . . I can see him so plainly . . . He's talking about the police for some reason.

SUSAN: They came to take statements for the inquest reports because he'd only been in hospital twenty-four hours.

DORIS: I see, because he was saying, the police came, you know. I was very important . . . I expect you were, darling. Now, who's Anne . . . A . . . A no it's not, it's Alan.

SUSAN: My brother-in-law.

DORIS: He says Alan was in our house, Granny Doris. He came back so I did a bit of good.

SUSAN: Yes, we hadn't seen him for years.

DORIS: Now, who's Rose . . . R . . . R it's an R . . . sound. Hold it, hold hold it, don't get yourself fussed, lovey. Well, I am listening, Simon, honestly I am, but you keep bobbing about, first to your mummy, then to your daddy . . . Richard it is! Richard!

SUSAN: Yes, next door.

120

DORIS: He said, Richard, will you listen. I used to play with Richard, he was my best friend when we weren't falling out!

SUSAN: Yes!

DORIS: He used to say I'm not friends with you any more, but do you know, Richard cried and he brought me a little bunch of flowers.

SUSAN: Yes, he did.

DORIS: 'Cos they stand and watch. He says there were so many people there. Margaret was there. Who's Margaret?

SUSAN: Richard's mummy.

DORIS: He says yes, they all cried. Richard was my best friend and we used to take it in turns on my bike. So you only had one bike between you, did you?

SUSAN: Yes, in our garden.

DORIS: And Margaret cried and do you know what she said to my mummy? She said, It could so easily have been me.

SUSAN: Yes, that's what she said.

DORIS: Now, there's somebody called George on the spirit side . . . I think he belongs with your father, love.

SUSAN: Oh, his brother George.

DORIS: George is here when he can get a word in with young Simon. He's telling me there was a great hoo-hah and they still haven't been able to find a satisfactory answer as to why it happened, but he says it doesn't really matter, now, does it. Simon's here, he's happy, he's full of joy . . . Who's Betty?

SUSAN: Aunty Betty.

DORIS: Betty loves me, he says she's got a picture of me and she puts roses by it.

SUSAN: Yes, she does.

DORIS: She puts them down and says those are for you

Simon . . . Now, George is saying he knows what the problem is. You are worried because you felt you couldn't say goodbye to him. And you blame yourself, love, we all do it, believe me. There's not a parent comes into my house, including me, that doesn't ask themself was there anything I could have done? Should I have noticed anything? Should I have insisted on having another doctor? Should I have done this, should I have done that? We all go through it, love. But there was nothing you could have done . . . He was one of God's special children . . . Now, March the seventeenth is important.

SUSAN: March sixteenth was the day he died.

DORIS: Why they are telling you this is that when March sixteenth comes round you're not to say it's a year since our Simon died. You must give him some flowers and say happy anniversary, love. Because it'll be the anniversary of the first year of his new life . . . Who's Tony? It's a T sound. Tony, Terry, Tommy . . . No, you've missed it Simon. Now hold it. What are you showing me? He's taken his shirt off and here, on his shoulder blade he's got a little mole.

SUSAN: Yes.

DORIS: I said you're not going to strip off, are you? And he said no only my shirt to show Mummy that it's me . . . Now there's a J . . . Jamey . . . no, Jenny.

SUSAN: That's his friend's mum.

DORIS: What about a caravan, love? I've just been talking about a caravan but you know a caravan too?

SUSAN: Yes, his grandpa's caravan. He lives in a caravan. We've just been there.

DORIS: Well, he went with you . . . You see, for a child like Simon who was eight when he went over, to suddenly find himself having to live somewhere else with people he didn't know before was a great shock, so they let him come back and see you and join in with what you're doing. And he says we went to the caravan, you know. We did. And I, I-I-I-I . . . He stutters when he gets excited.

SUSAN: Yes, he did.

DORIS: He's getting so excited his tongue trips over itself. At the caravan there's four steps, you know, and we've been going there since Mummy had to lift me down but now I'm a big boy and I walk up and down them myself.

SUSAN: Yes, we've been going there since he was very small.

DORIS: And he says he still goes and cuddles his teddy.

SUSAN: No, we put the teddy in with him.

DORIS: Oh, I see you've got your teddy with you . . . I thought you meant you came and played with it . . . And you've got that other . . . elephant, is it? Funny-looking thing. I don't know what you call that? Your Wopple?

SUSAN: Womble.

DORIS: Now he's saying something about a guitar. I thought he said his daddy promised him a guitar when he's a big boy.

SUSAN: He always loved guitars. He had a little wooden one. Mark's got it now.

DORIS: I was going to have a proper one when I was a big boy, he's saying.

SUSAN: Yes, he used to talk about playing in a pop group.

DORIS: There's Mark his brother, then there's someone called Michael and someone called Nicolas.

SUSAN: His friends.

DORIS: Yes . . . and . . . Wait a minute, darling, wait a minute. Simon, love, off you go again, I can't keep

123

up with you. Tell me again. Yes, you had your teddy with you, yes and you had your womble. Now, what are you telling me? He's putting my hand over, like that. So you put something in his hand. Did you say a photograph?

SUSAN: Yes, I put a photo of the two boys in his hand.

DORIS: That's it, because he folded my fingers over and said it's a picture ... And he twists his hair round. All the time he's talking to me he's twisting his hair ... Do you drive for a living, Philip?

PHILIP: No, but I drive a long way to work.

DORIS: Oh, 'cos he said I drive with Daddy, you know. A long way we go. So that's what made me ask if you drive for a living. Oh, he's saying no, Daddy's got a big machine, he's ever so clever.

PHILIP: Yes, I work in a factory.

DORIS: Now ... slowly, slowly, Simon. He won't let George do it. He will do it himself. Now, you know your sitting-room. It used to be two rooms.

SUSAN: The house where he was born was like that.

DORIS: And then the wall came down. Now, where you live now I'm facing a glass door and there's a picture on the right of him and a picture on the left, too.

SUSAN: There used to be a picture on the right but I took it down and now there's just the one on the left.

DORIS: Had he just had a watch?

SUSAN: Yes, just before Christmas.

DORIS: It's a proper watch, he says. Mark's got that now. He's talking about Christopher.

SUSAN: Christopher sat next to him at school.

DORIS: And there's a little chair that he used to take out in the garden.

SUSAN: Yes, a fold-up one.

DORIS: He says I used to go and sit out in the garden

with Mummy and I had my own little chair . . . Oh, you didn't! Now, just a minute, let the grown-ups show me a picture, darling . . . You've got me a bit lost now because you get very excited. Now, there are kitchen units and they look like pale olive green.

SUSAN: That's Lynne, next door but one.

DORIS: That's where he's taking me and there's a chopping board or a tray or something, on these units. He said I knocked it down.

SUSAN: Yes, he did.

DORIS: He's done it since he's been over to let you know he's there.

SUSAN: She blames it on Gary.

DORIS: No, it's Simon. He says it makes ever such a bang. And then he's talking about a dog.

SUSAN: Poppy.

DORIS: The dog can see me but they can't see me. That puzzles him . . . You know when he was born, the cord wasn't round his neck, was it?

SUSAN: It was round Mark's.

DORIS: Oh, that was Mark, was it. He says the cord was round his neck and he nearly died, but then he didn't and it was me . . . Now he said he had a money box and that's been opened and d'you know how much was in it? There was nearly £4.

SUSAN: Yes, he was saving for his Lego fire station.

DORIS: I only wanted two more pounds then I could have had it.

SUSAN: Yes, he could.

DORIS: £6 it was. You see they don't forget. He's still your child even though you can't see him . . . Oh, he's disappeared now. I don't know where he's gone . . . It's all right, he's back. No, I'm here, he said and I asked where he'd been and he said I've been to fetch Elsie.

SUSAN: Elsie lived over the road. She's only just gone.

DORIS: Did she have a stroke? Because Simon says she had a head thing too.

SUSAN: Yes, she did.

DORIS: Elsie says to tell you that your little boy is more beautiful than ever. She used to see him every day. He used to go down to post a letter because there's a letter box at the end of the road.

SUSAN: Yes, there is.

DORIS: Now they're talking about someone called David.

SUSAN: Yes, he lives next door.

DORIS: Then there's Mark and Lesley and Geoffrey.

SUSAN: His cousins, but he didn't know them.

DORIS: He does now . . . And he used to love pink blancmange I heard him say . . . Now, who's Maisie? Think of your mum. Is there a Maisie or Mabel connected with her?

PHILIP: Yes, Auntie Mabel.

DORIS: Somebody called Arthur.

SUSAN: That's my side.

DORIS: And somebody's got a van, I thought he said.

SUSAN: We've just got a funny little car. A Panda.

DORIS: It's not a van, love, it's a Panda. Oh, I thought it was a van, he says. It's not like the other cars we had.

SUSAN: No, it's not. It's square, like a little box van.

DORIS: Now, that's Irene or Eileen living. I have to give you both because they sound alike to me.

SUSAN: Irene.

DORIS: Then there's Kathleen.

SUSAN: Katy. It should be Kathleen but we call her Katy.

DORIS: His birthday's just gone, there's another one in August and one in October.

SUSAN: Yes, mine.

126

DORIS: Now, what is it you're telling me? Just before you went to the spirit world you had a new red sweater?

SUSAN: Yes, he had a new red sweater. He was buried in his favourite red shirt.

DORIS: You can ask me about it, he's saying, I don't mind because I'm here. They've told me about it. It's only like a garden in memory of Simon. There's a tree there, and roses planted.

SUSAN: Yes.

DORIS: When Mummy and Daddy go there I try to tell them please don't cry because it's only my garden. I'm not there. Can you tell me where you come from? All I've got written down in my book is 'child' . . . I thought he said Chester.

SUSAN: Winchester.

DORIS: December the ninth, I think he said. No? Could it have been September, November. No, I'm guessing at it. Let it go Simon, love. I think you've done extremely well. Do you think I look like my daddy, he's asking. Yes I do, love, and your mummy too. He's got your eyes, Susan, that's for sure . . . Well, I've got to get washed and changed now, love. You've done extremely well.

I know it was a terrible blow to you, love, losing him so quickly. But at least it was over in a few hours. He didn't suffer. Not like some of these parents whose children have leukaemia and they have to watch them suffer for years . . .

Anyway, I'll make you some more tea . . .

Well, as you can see, there is nothing eerie about a sitting. It's just a three-way conversation filled with trivial little bits of family information. Not much in themselves, but important to the people concerned because they are things that only the loved one could have known, described in the language that he used to use.

There is such a difference in the way sitters arrive and the way they leave. Particularly the parents who've lost children. They walk in droopy and desolate, hope almost gone. And you should see the way they go out. Heads held high, the spring back in their step because suddenly they can face the future.

# CHAPTER 8

It was cold, very cold, and all around me the world was exploding. Smoke blurred my vision, there were voices shouting, great flashes lit up the sky and crashes like thunder shook the ground under my feet.

Half-deafened and confused, I stumbled about, then there was a tremendous bang and everything went blank. I had a last vague impression of pulling something over me, of covering myself and then there was silence.

So began one of the strangest cases I have ever worked on. I have no real explanation for it even today. Yet it happened and I faithfully recorded every detail. It puzzles me still.

The above scene was shown to me as the last impression of Philip Alan Williams, a young soldier missing, presumed dead in the Falklands War. His parents had attended a memorial service for him in their local church and they were invited to the official memorial service at St Paul's Cathedral. But still they grieved and in desperation they wrote to me.

I had a very busy schedule but they sounded so unhappy I went against my normal family rule and agreed to see them on Sunday afternoon. Usually I try to leave weekends free unless I have church work to do because the older I get the more rest I seem to need. Psychic contact seems to be very physically draining.

Anyway, the Williams's arrived and I was glad I'd broken my weekend rule. We had a marvellous sitting. Philip Alan came through and gave a mass of information about his family, along with quite a few private, personal details that no one, apart from his closest friends and family, could have known. He described the place where he was last seen, the people he was with and the terrifying events going on – all with great accuracy as we discovered afterwards.

Yet unknown to us, as his parents were speeding down the motorway to London, halfway across the world in the Falklands Philip was walking into a house in Goose Green. He was cold, half starved and exhausted. He was given a meal and put to bed by the kind family and, at the time of our sitting, he was not on the other side, but in a deep, exhausted sleep.

So how did it happen? I've got no definite answer. My only theory is that the part of us that lives on after death, the spirit, is naturally present within us when we're alive and in some circumstances it can leave the body during deep sleep, travel about and return to the body before the sleeper wakes. These travels are sometimes remembered afterwards as a dream.

I realize this might sound far-fetched but it would explain the many cases you hear about where a person 'dreams' of going to visit a close relative or friend and finds them ill, only to discover the next day that that person really is ill.

I believe that in Philip's case he was anxious about his parents, knowing that they must have feared the worst, and when he slept, his 'spirit' restlessly came in search of them to give them reassurance.

The psychic 'pull' must have been very strong when you consider that the three of us, his mother, father and me, were sitting there concentrating all our energies on contacting Philip, willing him to come and talk to us. The power generated must have shone out like a beacon on the astral plane and guided him straight to my living-room even though it was half a world away.

I cannot prove this theory of course but one little

remark after the event makes me think I'm right. During the sitting Philip mentioned something about his father having bought a new car. Now, he would not have known about this in the normal way because his father didn't get it until after Philip had sailed for the Falklands. Yet the person I was talking to mentioned the car. Very puzzling. Then when Philip finally arrived home from his ordeal his father proudly showed him the car but Philip didn't seem surprised.

'It's funny, Dad,' he said, 'but while I was away I had a funny dream. I can't remember it all but I remember I dreamed you'd got a new car – and you have.'

To me, that proves Philip was able to reach out to his parents from thousands of miles away even though he dismissed the experience as a dream.

That's my theory anyway but I'll put down the whole story and you can make up your own mind whether you agree with me.

The Williams's arrived, as arranged, having driven hundreds of miles for a one-hour sitting. The poor things must have been worn out so we put the kettle on to make them some tea, but even as I was crossing the hall I heard the name Goose Green.

Anyone who followed the Falklands War will know that Goose Green figured very heavily in all the reports about it, so I could be accused of guessing. Nevertheless, I heard the words so clearly and distinctly I was sure they were significant.

'Your son didn't go missing at Goose Green, did he?' I asked the parents.

They shook their heads. 'No. He wasn't involved in that, Doris,' they said firmly.

I was puzzled. I knew this wasn't a mistake because it was too clear, but if they said the boy hadn't been to Goose Green, then he hadn't.

It was only the next day we learned that even as we were talking Philip had turned up in Goose Green.

Anyway we sat down in the living-room, tea-cups within reach and I was about to tune in, when an odd feeling began to nag at me. There was something not quite right here.

'Are you quite sure your son's been killed?' I asked them.

'Oh, yes,' they said. 'We were invited to the memorial service at St Paul's and everything.'

'He couldn't have been taken prisoner?' I queried.

'No,' they said firmly. 'We were told there were no prisoners.'

I bit my lip. It was quite wrong of me to go on like this. I could be planting cruel seeds of hope in their minds when there was no sense in hoping. The Army were quite sure Philip was dead and they should know. The parents seemed to have accepted the fact and that was the best thing for them. It would be very wrong to unsettle them now. And yet . . .

Firmly I stamped on this rebel instinct and tuned in. I was instantly reassured. A young, male voice came straight in and gave the name Philip Alan. Called Alan for his Dad.

'Yes, that's Philip,' said his mother.

He gave his father's name, his sister's name and the name of a great friend of his.

'They've had a letter from Jimmy,' he said. 'And Stewart came to see them and they talked about me.'

His parents were astonished.

'Yes, that's true.'

Then he told me about himself. He chuckled and said he was a handsome lad, he had fair hair and he was trying to grow a moustache.

'Oh, I don't know about the moustache,' said his mother.

But Philip, if Philip it was, was adamant that he was trying to grow one.

He mentioned more family names and friends and asked to be remembered to various people, but he seemed unusually confused about which side some of his family were on. Occasionally a person making his first communication gets a little mixed up but in Philip this confusion was very strong. He would talk of people he'd met as if they were on the other side. Yet his parents would assure me that while these names were correct the people concerned were very much still with us.

Albert and Kitty were a typical example. He said something about meeting Albert and Kitty.

'But he couldn't have done,' said his father in dismay. 'Albert and Kitty are still alive. I was only talking to them the other day.'

'Philip, love, d'you mean you met Albert and Kitty or your father met Albert and Kitty?' I asked. He mumbled something about his father meeting them.

'Well, you must make it clear what side they're on, darling, or we'll get in a right mess. I thought you meant they were with you on that side.'

There was a strange scrambling of the vibration and a strong sense of confusion. Philip couldn't seem to understand what I meant. Abruptly he changed the subject.

'I didn't want to go you know,' he said. 'When I joined I never thought there'd be a war. On the way out we were laughing and joking but underneath we were scared . . .' I can't print the word he used but let's just say that Philip's language was just as rich as it always had been.

His mother nodded sadly. 'No, he didn't want to go,' she said. 'That's quite true.'

But he hadn't finished. He wanted them to know that,

although he had been frightened at the beginning, he hadn't been a coward.

'At least me mum and dad can be proud of me. I found me guts in the end. When it came to it you don't have time to think, you just go straight in.'

Then another voice interrupted, a young woman's voice.

'I'm Barbara,' she said. 'You mustn't worry about Philip. We're looking after him. He's all right.'

'That's his aunt,' said Mrs Williams.

Barbara said she was only in her thirties when she passed. She had been ill for some time but at the end it was very quick.

'I just went to sleep and woke up over here,' she said.

But Philip wasn't going to let Barbara take up much time. In the background I could hear organ music and Philip wanted to talk about his memorial service.

'They played *The Lord is My Shepherd* and lots of people came,' he said.

'I gave our Gareth a watch before I went away and he's still got it.'

He was also concerned about the pay still outstanding for the time he was in the Falklands. He wanted his father to chase it up.

'I earned the bugger,' he said, 'so you might as well have it.'

But Barbara was back. 'Don't you worry,' she said again. 'He'll be all right.'

Then yet another voice came in.

'I'm Elizabeth,' she said.

'That's his grandmother,' said Mrs Williams.

And she too was anxious to reassure them. 'Don't worry, we're looking after him.'

Listening to the tape afterwards I was struck by this constant reassurance. Relatives often like to let parents know that they are caring for the lost child who is now happy and well on the other side, but I have never heard it stressed so often during one sitting.

'Don't worry. He's all right. We're looking after him.' I heard it again and again. At the time I supposed that Mrs Williams must be particularly worried about Philip because his body had never been found and she didn't know he had died. Afterwards of course I realized that Philip's aunt and grandmother were not merely reassuring us but trying to tell us what was happening. They certainly were looking after Philip and he *was* all right. There was no need to worry.

Philip was not going to let his grandmother have any more of a say than his aunt. Back he came again as soon as Elizabeth finished speaking. He mentioned the new car, then he said, 'Dad's been talking to Joe Bailey. He works with him.'

Mr Williams nearly fell off his chair.

'Joe Bailey. Yes, that's right. I have,' he said. But then he remembered what he most wanted to know.

'Can he tell us what happened and where?' he asked.

'Can you give me your last impressions, Philip?' I asked. Again there was that strange scrambled sensation. A feeling of confusion and bewilderment. Then came the nightmare battle scene and a name.

'Temple something,' I said. 'Tem, tum . . .'

'Tumbledown,' said his father. 'That's right.'

Philip was getting agitated. 'There were all these explosions and then boof! That was it.' It sounded as if he had probably stepped on a landmine or been caught as one exploded.

'Chalky White was there and Anderson . . .' he added.

'Yes,' cried Mrs Williams. 'We had a letter from Sergeant White's widow, and Anderson *was* there too.'

'I was in the Guards,' said Philip.

135

His parents confirmed that he was indeed in the Scots Guards.

'How old are you, love?' I asked.

'Almost nineteen,' he replied.

Again this was correct. Yet suddenly that peculiar feeling was back, something was not right. What on earth was it?

'Well, I don't know,' I said aloud. 'If it's not Philip I'm talking to, how does he know all these things? It must be him.'

His parents were quite convinced of it. The way he talked. The occasional swear words he used and the information he gave were absolutely in character.

Yet the very next morning the news came through that Philip was alive. He was safe and well after living rough for several weeks. When he arrived home he was dressed in Chalky White's clothes, his own having been in an appalling state after weeks in the wild. He had also grown a moustache.

There had been a terrific explosion, he said, and he didn't remember any more until he found himself wandering alone in the bleak Falklands countryside. Thinking he was behind the Argentine lines and would therefore be taken prisoner if he was caught, he laid low until, at last, the bitter winter weather forced him to seek help.

His parents were overjoyed and when they phoned to tell me the good news I was delighted for them. But I was also mystified. If Philip was alive then who had I been talking to during the sitting? Could it have been one of the other young men who was killed that day? But no, the details were too personal to Philip. Could it have been Barbara? Again I had to dismiss the possibility. Barbara had turned up later in the sitting and was definitely a new voice. What's more Barbara's voice was unmistakably feminine while the person I'd thought was Philip was unmistakably a young man.

The only conclusion I could come to was that somehow I had been talking to Philip, even though Philip was not dead.

So how did it happen? Well, as I've said, I've got my theory but I wouldn't insist it was right or force it on anyone else. I'll leave you to make up your own mind.

Philip Alan Williams however wasn't my only contact with the Falklands War. Soon after my sitting with his parents another set of distraught parents telephoned me. Marion and Don Pryce had lost their son, a Fleet Air Arm electrician, when his ship the *Atlantic Conveyor* had been hit by an Exocet missile.

Soon after the disaster, the Pryces' daughter, who was a nurse, accidentally knocked a book on the floor when she was looking for something else at the hospital where she worked. Irritably she picked it up and saw that it was called *Voices in my Ear*. Something about the cheerful yellow cover attracted her interest and although she was in a hurry she turned the book over and read the little introduction on the back.

It was enough to convince her that the book might contain something that would help ease the terrible sense of loss the whole family was suffering, so she took the book home. It was passed rapidly to every member of the family and when they'd finished it they went out and got the sequel, *More Voices*. At the end of that Marion phoned me.

I was still feeling bewildered over the Philip Williams case but I couldn't refuse the Pryces'. Something in Marion's voice told me I had to see her. The Pryces were a very close family, it turned out, and all five of them arrived on my doorstep. Mother, father, and three pretty daughters. It was a pleasure to see such a lovely family and, though our small sitting-room looked rather over-crowded, I enjoyed it immensely.

I'd always wanted a big family myself and though it wasn't to be I still enjoy the company of other people's families.

We chatted for a few moments then I felt the presence of a young man. He was a tall, slim lad with thick hair and the sort of friendly, open face that immediately attracts people and invites their trust. As he hovered close to me I felt compelled to touch my hair with my fingers.

Marion gasped. 'That's our son! That's what he used to do. He used to touch his hair just like that!'

'I'm Don,' said the boy. 'And there are two Dons over here now. Me and my grandad.'

At that an elderly male voice interrupted.

'Yes, he was named after me, not his father. We used to be called the Three Dons.'

I asked the youngest Don what had happened to him. Immediately I could smell fire. I could see flames licking around and I could hear a lot of shouting.

'I was helping some of the others to get overboard,' said Don, 'and I think my life jacket caught fire. When I jumped into the sea it went down.'

He was drowned very quickly, but at least he didn't suffer for hours in the icy cold waters of the South Atlantic.

But Don didn't want to dwell on the war. He changed the subject and talked instead of his friend Danny and his girlfriend Sarah.

'I think I would have married Sarah,' he said, 'if it hadn't been for the war. Just before I went, you know, Mum took me out to buy me some new things. She bought me some underpants.'

'Yes, that's true, I did,' said Marion.

He went on to give more family names and he said that

his sister had some pictures on the wall over the fireplace which he had given her, that his parents had a crucifix on their bedroom wall and that he'd given his youngest sister a soft toy. He also mentioned Mr Bond, his scoutmaster.

'Oh yes, he was a very keen scout,' said Don senior.

Then the grandfather came back.

'I died of cancer of the lungs,' he said, 'but there's no need to be sad. It was a happy release to go.'

'Is Don happy with you all over there?' I asked.

Don's voice came back. 'Not yet,' he said sadly, 'I miss you still.'

The power was fading but with a last effort he muttered something about 'Flowers and a message of love'.

There was a pause. 'Roses,' he added.

This didn't mean much to his family.

'Did you give him roses by his picture or at the memorial service?' I suggested.

But no, the Pryces couldn't think of anything that seemed likely. However the day of the sitting was 4 August. Afterwards they discovered that on 30 July their next-door neighbour had dropped a wreath made of silk roses from his helicopter into the sea around the Falklands with a message of love for Don and all those who had lost their lives there.

I never thought I'd live long enough to see Britain involved in another war or that I'd one day work for parents and wives who were suffering the way we suffered in World War II.

I know from bitter experience about the tragedy of war. There were the weeks of heartache when I was informed my husband was missing, presumed dead at Arnhem. Then the anxious months when I discovered that he'd been found but he was a prisoner of war and seriously injured.

Long before that I lost the boyfriend I hoped to marry

when his plane was shot down. I'd met John Stewart at a dance. He was a rear gunner in the Air Force, a tall fair-haired boy from Scotland.

He was kind and thoughtful and he was the first person to buy me an Easter egg. It was a big one with roses on it and I was thrilled. It was typical of John.

We had been going out together for eighteen months when we decided to make it permanent. He was stationed in Huntingdon at the time and I was in Wales and he wrote to ask me if I would meet him at Grantham so that we could visit my mother. Afterwards he said we could travel up to Scotland to meet his parents and buy an engagement ring.

I thought this was a wonderful idea and I dashed off to apply for a forty-eight-hour pass. Yet as I handed over my request a voice seemed to say in my head.

'You're not going to go.'

This sobered me up a bit. Oh, I suppose they'll turn me down, I thought. I was convinced that if I wasn't going it was because something my end would prevent it.

The pass was granted, however, and I forgot all about those warning words. Then on the Thursday before we were due to leave a bulky packet arrived for me. It contained the letters I'd written to John, with a note to say that he had been killed.

The terrible thing about war is how quickly it can flare up. In the case of the Falklands conflict it was over very quickly too, yet for hundreds of people those few weeks changed their lives for ever and they will never be completely happy again. They will carry sadness in their hearts – for as long as they live.

Violence isn't confined to war. It seems to spill over into everyday life and I get an increasing number of cases these days involving ordinary people who've met violent senseless deaths.

I've asked Ramanov about this and he says it's because we don't love each other enough. That until we learn to love each other more and not to expect more from people than they're capable of giving, then these things will happen.

I expect that's true but I still don't understand what makes one person lash out at another. I mean what makes a man beat the woman he's supposed to love so savagely that he smashes her bones? It doesn't make sense. All I can do is try to comfort the other victims, the ones who are left to grieve when the violence goes too far.

The case of Shirley X (I won't give her full name because she doesn't want her children to know the whole story) is a particularly horrifying example. Her mother came to see me because she was desperate to know more about what had happened to her daughter.

Shirley came through quickly enough but she was full of regrets. She couldn't settle until she'd told her mother how sorry she was for the mess she'd made.

'I threw my life away at thirty-three,' she said, and as she came close my whole body seemed to ache and there was a burning pain in my stomach.

'I suffered very badly,' she said. 'I couldn't have taken much more. I tried so hard to stay but it was no use.'

'Shirley, can you give me your last impression, love?' I asked. She said she went under and then I felt a falling sensation as if I'd been thrown. It was difficult to make out what was happening.

'I wasn't killed outright,' Shirley explained. 'I suffered.'

At first I couldn't see her, but I could feel that her hair swung down round her shoulders. Then she appeared by her mother and I realized she was a strikingly beautiful girl, with film star looks.

'Now, how can I describe your hair, Shirley?' I asked. 'You're not blonde and you're not auburn.'

141

'You could say sandy, I suppose,' she replied, but she was being modest. Her hair was a lovely natural golden colour.

'We used to call it honey blonde,' said her mother.

She mentioned the names of her ex-husband and her two children who lived with him. She talked of her grandad and dozens of other relatives and friends.

Then she mentioned a man's name.

'That was the person who was supposed to be her friend who lived in the same block of flats,' said her mother.

'Hah hah,' said Shirley when she heard this. 'Friend!'

She sighed. 'I didn't want to say because I didn't want to upset Mum, but it was him. He threw me and belted me and I hadn't got a lot left to make me look nice after the divorce but all I had was taken. My jewellery, rings and watches, everything was taken.'

'Yes,' said her mother, 'he stole them.'

'And now he's walking free,' Shirley added bitterly. 'You see, my mum and dad helped me so much over my husband and I'd been a real trial to my parents. I've got to be honest about myself, and then I made another big mistake and I was too bloody proud to go and say I've made a mistake, can you get me out of it. It cost me my life. Can you understand why I couldn't go to them when I should? I'm very proud, an arrogant young bitch and I couldn't face telling them.'

'That's the way she speaks,' I added hastily, in case her mother thought I was being insulting.

'Oh yes, that's all right. I know.'

Shirley went on to tell me she promoted things for a living.

'Yes, she did a lot of demonstrations,' said her mother.

'I made a very good living but I was so stupid, I always fell for the takers, not the givers. He was very cruel to me. He was evil, yet he had a fascination for me.'

142

She was worried about her sister who had had a nervous breakdown over the tragedy, and she was full of remorse.

'I lived in a slum and it was a slum, Doris,' she said. 'I came from a good home, a good clean home yet I just couldn't . . . I don't know. I'm so sorry for all the heartache I caused my parents, but my kids will be all right. As far as they're concerned I just died and that was it, but please God they never find out about the rats and the state my body was in.'

Her mother explained that Shirley had been dead for three months when she finally got the police to break into the flat and her body was a mass of fractures and broken bones.

'My ex-husband was upset when he heard,' said Shirley. 'There was no real bad feeling between us, we were just not compatible. He wanted a home bird and I was never a home bird. That was the main problem. Now he's got a wife who's content to stay at home.'

In the end her life was so unpleasant Shirley said she was glad to have gone to the other side.

'I was scared stiff of him,' she said. 'He wouldn't let me out of the flat. Before the last beating he fractured my femur and I never did get to the hospital. I was glad to be out of it.'

Afterwards her mother told me that they tried everything to get Shirley away from this man but she would never come. They even paid for a taxi and sent it to the door but it returned empty. Letters and phone calls went unanswered and when they tried to visit her this man wouldn't let them in. She was ill, he would say, the place was a mess and Shirley didn't want to see them.

Eventually they were able to convince the police that this wasn't merely a family dispute, that they felt there was serious cause for alarm, but by then it was too late. Shirley had been dead for three months, this man had

143

pawned her jewellery and withdrawn the money from her building society account. He spent a short time in a mental hospital but there wasn't enough evidence to convict him of murder.

I came across another dreadful case like this quite by chance. I'd been asked to take part in a radio phone-in on Capital Radio.

It was the sort of show where listeners ring the studio and I try to get a few details for them over the phone line. This is more difficult than working with the sitter close to you but sometimes you get very good results.

The phone was going non stop and the programme was flowing with the usual loving messages, when a male caller was put through to me. At once I heard the name Susan, which turned out to be the name of his daughter, then there was a terrible pressure round my neck. I was choking for breath. Shocked, I realized that this girl had been strangled. But how could I say that over the air?

'This girl should not have died,' I croaked, my throat still dry from the unpleasant experience. 'She went over very quickly. It shouldn't have happened. Do you understand what I mean?'

The man assured me he did. There were a few more family details and then I was urged to move on to the next caller. Reluctantly I had to leave the bereaved father but I hoped he would contact me privately.

He did. Soon after the show I got a phone call asking if I could possibly see Mr and Mrs Chalkley, whose daughter, Susan, had spoken to them through me on the phone-in.

Apparently the case had been in the papers while I was away in Australia. Susan had been strangled by her lover who then set fire to the house in an effort to get rid of the body, even though Susan's small daughter was still inside.

Susan couldn't rest because she was so angry about

144

this and because she was upset by the things that people were saying about her. She didn't mind for herself but she couldn't bear to see what it was doing to her parents.

'It was the first time, Mum, I don't care what anyone says, it was the first time. Believe me,' she cried.

'I was living apart from my husband and I was going to get a divorce and then this had to happen. I know my parents worry that I suffered a lot but I didn't. I was unconscious almost immediately.'

The gossip that always surrounds such cases was still on her mind. 'I know what people have said but I didn't keep a bad house,' Susan sobbed. 'It was the first time, before God, on my baby's life, that I'd ever gone to bed with somebody.

'I don't know what I was thinking of. I was lonely and fed up and look what happened. But I wouldn't want them to think badly of me. We were brought up decently.'

She mentioned a few family names and remembered her grandmother and her two sisters' birthdays.

'I was the middle one of the family,' she explained. Yet she was still sad.

'There's been so much aggravation since it happened over my baby,' she said and her mother nodded. 'He didn't want to know about our Mandy before, so what the hell does he want to start now for? Now I've gone and my sister and my family have stepped in and said they want her, he's suddenly said he wants her.'

I paused for breath. Susan was getting very cross, and it was difficult to keep up with her.

'Presumably she's talking about her husband,' I said.

'Yes,' said Mrs Chalkley. 'That's right, but Mandy is very happy and well looked after by her father.'

Susan calmed down at this.

'Oh, she's beautiful, my little girl,' she told me. 'She's got big eyes and a fringe across her forehead . . .' Her voice changed again. 'You see it was in the bedroom. Then there was the bathroom and Mandy was in the room next to the bathroom. The bastard set a fire, you know. Thank goodness the bathroom was in between my bedroom and where Amanda was. The bastard . . . You see I used to go out, I won't pretend I didn't, but I didn't bring men home to sleep with me.'

She was starting to upset herself again, so to change the subject I asked her for some more details about her family.

She mentioned the boy who used to run errands for her, she talked of Whitley Bay where she'd spent many happy holidays as a child and then she spat another name.

'Dickinson.'

'That's the name of the man who did it,' said her father.

Finally as the power faded, she made a last effort to help her mother.

'Mum, you're going to stop taking those tablets now, aren't you?'

Mrs Chalkley crumbled. 'I've already tried to stop but I can't,' she sobbed. 'I go down so much.'

'Oh, tell her she must,' Susan begged me.

'They're not doing you any good, love,' I said. 'Susan does so want you to stop. She tells me you still feel guilty inside but it's not your fault. You think if you'd taken a bit more interest, maybe she wouldn't have got married when she did, or maybe the marriage would have worked. But there was nothing you could have done. She is a very strong-willed girl and she'd made up her mind.'

Susan, of course, had not changed a bit. She hadn't become a little angel now she was on the other side. She was still strong-willed and she was still angry about what had happened to her.

This is often the case. Possibly after years on the other side people learn saintly forgiveness and tolerance, but

146

those who feel rushed over before their time remain angry for quite a while.

Stephen Peace, for example, was only nineteen when he was killed in a motor-cycle accident. He was a very good rider and had passed an advanced motor-cycling test, yet his skills couldn't help him escape a fatal accident. He was very sad because it happened at an exciting moment in his life.

'Julie and I were going to get engaged,' he said. 'On Julie's seventeenth birthday. I loved her very much, as she loved me, and I still love her.'

Everything was going well for him when one day he rode down Market Street he said, near his home.

'I was riding down the road when this woman pulled out in front of me. She did a U-turn without looking. I tried to avoid her, I turned the bike hard, but it was no use. I went into her sideways.

'And do you know,' he added furiously, 'that bloody bitch got away with it!'

He was anxious about Julie.

'She can't forget me,' he said. 'But I want her to be happy. I want her to go out with other people. She's so pretty. Her hair comes down to her shoulders and it flicks up at the ends. She always wears T-shirts. Even in the winter.'

Fred and Pat Peace, Stephen's parents, agreed that all he said was true and, hearing them, Stephen seemed to calm down. I've noticed that the one thing that helps these angry people is to get their grievance off their chests.

'Oh well,' he finished. 'Mum always said "That bloody bike, it's a bloody death-trap." If only I'd listened to her.'

# CHAPTER 9

Early one spring morning in 1982, Waiter 25 clocked silently into the Pizza Inc Restaurant in Swallow Street, London.

He punched his number into the special clocking-in device on the till, which automatically recorded it, along with the date and the time. It was 20 March and the time was 6.54 a.m.

But when the owners, Richard and Barbara Possner, arrived an hour later at 8.00, the place was deserted, the doors were still locked and bolted just as they were left the night before, the burglar alarms were undisturbed and the till was switched off because the Possners possess the only key to switch it on.

Of Waiter 25 there was no sign. But then that didn't surprise them. They don't have a Waiter 25.

'The thing is, Doris,' said Richard Possner when he telephoned me several weeks later, 'it's just not possible. I mean, without the till key you can't record anything on the till. It just won't work. There is only one key, which Barbara and I keep for security reasons, and it was with us that morning in our flat.

'What's more, forgetting the key for a moment, we know someone must have been in the restaurant at 6.54 a.m. but how did he get in and out without setting off the alarms or breaking any of the locks?'

It was a mystery all right but this incident alone hadn't driven them to seek help. It was only when strange things were happening with such regularity that the staff were getting uneasy that the Possners realized something would have to be done.

There was the burglar alarm, for instance. The bell was situated inside the restaurant high up on a wall where no one could reach it without a ladder. So, when during a routine test the Possners discovered it wasn't working, they called in a specialist.

'When he opened up the bell he found a stone wedged inside it, breaking the circuit,' said Barbara. 'He said in all his experience he'd never seen anything so clever and he was used to dealing with the work of professional criminals. But even if a criminal had thought up the idea, how would he have got in to tamper with the bell? Richard and I keep the keys to the restaurant and you couldn't help noticing a man on a ladder messing about with the alarm.'

Then there was the clock. On the wall they had mounted a handsome station clock powered by an electric battery so that it didn't need winding. It was a lovely clock. Everyone admired it, but within days of coming to the restaurant it went wrong. No matter what anyone did, it would not go past twelve midnight. At midnight it stopped dead. In the end the Possners had to get rid of it.

But they couldn't get rid of everything. They needed the gas oven, for instance. Yet after a while even this became faulty. For no apparent reason the gas kept blowing out and nothing could be cooked. The engineers were called in and although they solved the problem, they deepened the mystery.

'They said they couldn't understand it at all,' said Richard. 'They said a hidden screw deep inside the oven had come unscrewed, but it wouldn't have done so on its own. Yet unless you were an expert on these particular ovens you wouldn't even know the screw was there, let alone know what it was for. You certainly couldn't see it by looking through the oven door.'

When they opened the freezer and found all the meat

149

defrosting because the switch had apparently turned itself off, they weren't even surprised so hardened had they become to the peculiarities of the restaurant.

The 'ghost', they told each other, had a weakness for gadgets. They began to feel they understood how his mind worked.

Well, they shouldn't have said that. Not aloud anyway. Because then he changed his tactics. One afternoon Richard walked into the restaurant and noticed a strong smell of gas. Several people complained about it and everyone could smell it.

Naturally assuming they had a leak, Richard telephoned the gas board. The emergency engineers arrived almost immediately. One sniff was enough to confirm that there was indeed a very bad smell of gas. Yet when they set up their instruments they could find no trace of a leak. After an exhaustive search of the area they were forced to give up, quite baffled.

It was around this time that Val, one of the waitresses, happened to be alone in the bar polishing glasses ready for the lunch-time customers.

'Val!' called a male voice.

She looked up, but no one was there. The restaurant and bar were quite empty. Impatiently she put down her cloth and went into the kitchen.

'Yes? What d'you want?'

The chef looked blank. 'Want? I don't want anything.'

'But you just called me, didn't you?'

'No, not me,' said the chef.

Puzzled, Val returned to the bar but there was no one there. She searched the store rooms and cupboard for signs of colleagues playing a joke, but found nothing. It was odd, that's all, and she would probably have forgotten about it had it not happened again, not once but several times.

Soon she was hearing her name called softly whenever she was working alone. It was always the same male voice but since he only said one short word, she couldn't get any clues to his identity. Age and accent were impossible to guess. At first Val found it merely irritating but as the weeks passed she began to get edgy. She wasn't frightened exactly but the place was beginning to give her the creeps.

It was some time before she mentioned it to the Possners. She felt a bit foolish, as if they would think she was going mad. But in the end it was so obvious there was something wrong she had to tell them. And of course they didn't laugh.

By now after six months at the restaurant they were convinced the place was haunted and they were beginning to take the ghost seriously.

They were both young, down-to-earth people, hard-working types who had never given such things a thought before, but this was different. It had reached the stage where the business they'd dreamed of for so long might be at risk.

'Could you come as soon as possible, Doris?' asked Richard. 'This afternoon if you like.'

I laughed. 'Oh dear, I'm afraid I can't come now, I've got somebody coming. What about Monday?'

'Okay. Monday,' said Richard.

And that's how, despite the fact that I was up to my eyes with cases involving children, I came to be sitting drinking tea the following Monday afternoon in a London restaurant.

It was a welcome relief from the pressure of work. These days I get so many thousands of requests for sittings that I have to turn away more than I can accept. For this reason I devote most of my time to bereaved parents because, rightly or wrongly, I believe they are the ones most in need of help.

151

The trouble is, this kind of work is the most emotionally draining of the lot and so, just occasionally, it's nice to get my teeth into a good old impersonal ghost.

Pizza Inc turned out to be a very nice, very unusual restaurant. The minute I walked through the door I could tell that there was nothing evil here. There was a warm, pleasant atmosphere and it felt, and looked, relaxing. The air of tranquillity might have had something to do with the fact that the place appeared to have been furnished with items discarded from churches.

There was stained glass in the windows, pews had been made into bench seats, there were bits of screens and altar rails and even a pulpit.

'Oh, isn't it lovely!' I exclaimed as we walked in.

'Glad you think so,' said Richard, looking pleased. 'We like it anyway.'

'Did all this stuff come from a church?'

He explained that it had been gathered from all over the place but a lot had come from old churches. He went off to get us a pot of tea and I stretched out in my chair.

'Well, this makes a change, doesn't . . .' I stopped and stared in amazement as a monk in a long brown robe walked past.

For a moment I thought they might be extending the ecclesiastical theme to the waiters and waitresses by dressing them as monks and nuns, but then I realized that this was a real monk and he'd passed over long ago.

As I watched he turned, and seemed to glide back past us but, as he drew level, he raised his head and gave us a smile of great serenity. Then he was gone.

Well, I thought to myself, there is a ghost here but he's not doing any harm, he's certainly not fiddling about with switches and making trouble. The monk is responsible for the feeling of peace and tranquillity. He likes to see his old things being put to good use and cared for.

All the same I was very surprised to have seen him. These days I rarely see adult spirits, I only see children. Occasionally an adult will appear, but hardly ever during a sitting. It's usually when I'm not tuned in and when I least expect it.

'Well, there's a monk here, I can tell you that,' I said to Richard as he came back with the tea. 'But it's not him. He's happy to come back now and again to see what you're doing with his stuff. No, there must be something else.'

But I could feel there was something complicated about this case, so I tuned in first to see if Richard's relatives could help. It was Richard's father, I think, who came through. He said how proud he was of Richard and that he had no need to worry because the restaurant was going to be a great success.

'Some of these incidents,' he said, 'are nothing to do with us. They are man-made. There is jealousy at work,' and he went on to name one or two members of staff who had recently left.

'These people had something to do with some of the incidents,' he said.

Richard agreed that he'd always been uneasy about one of the people named and was glad he'd gone.

However, even though some of the mysteries were of earthly origin, it was clear that others weren't. The next step was to find out where the spirit was operating from. Once we'd located him, we could talk to him.

In all these cases, the presence of the spirit is betrayed by a patch of freezing cold air. You have to walk slowly across the floor until you find the cold spot and, no matter how good the central heating, a cold spot will be there if there is a spirit present.

'Now,' I said to Richard and Barbara, 'I'm going to walk round the room and I want you to follow me, putting your feet in exactly the same place that I put my feet. All right?'

They thought it was rather funny but, laughing and chattering, we formed a little procession and wound slowly through the restaurant.

Richard had a feeling the problem might come from the kitchen, so we went there first.

Carefully I padded over every inch of the floor but there was nothing. The temperature was quite even.

'No, it's not here, Richard,' I said. We moved on to the store cupboard. Again, though it was chilly, it was the natural chill of a cool room not the unmistakable sensation of a cold spot in an otherwise normal room.

We backed into the restaurant again and I stepped carefully along the strip of lino behind the bar. Halfway along I stopped.

'I think I've found it.' The room was warm but just here, close to the beer taps, cold waves were rippling over me. Then I realized I was standing next to the ice bucket.

I laughed. 'No. It's probably a false alarm. I'm beside the ice bucket!'

Was it just the ice bucket? I wondered, or was there something else there? I couldn't be sure and unless I was certain I wouldn't say anything.

I returned to the main body of the restaurant. It was fairly large and we patiently pigeon-stepped up and down the aisles. At last, at the far end, I felt another wave of cold air. I stood still. Yes, definitely cold air.

'Barbara,' I said turning round, 'come and stand just here and tell me what you feel.'

I moved aside and Barbara took my place. She paused for a moment, head on one side.

'Yes, it's cold. Just here. It's peculiar.'

Then Richard glanced up.

'Hey, you're standing underneath the fan!'

I followed his gaze. There on the ceiling was one of those big old-fashioned blade fans.

'Oh dear, would you turn it off, Richard.'

Richard obligingly went to the switch. The fan stopped and I moved back to my original position. The cold was still welling up like bath water. The fan had made no difference.

'All right, Barbara,' I said, 'come back and we'll try it again.'

Barbara fitted her feet once more into the place I'd indicated.

'Yes, it's still here. It's the strangest thing.' Then she stopped. 'It seems to be going.'

'Going?' I echoed.

'Yes. Now it's gone.'

Quickly we changed places and I realized what she meant. The cold spot had gone and now the area was the same temperature as the rest of the room. This was very odd. Of course spirit entities can move around but since the aim of causing a disturbance is to draw attention to themselves they usually want to be found and they don't whisk about playing hide and seek.

'That is strange,' I said, but time was running out and we couldn't spend hours chasing an invisible ghost. The restaurant would be opening soon for the evening customers and I had to be finished by then.

'Well, never mind, let's see if he'll come and talk to us.'

We returned to our table from which the tea things had been cleared and I tuned in. There was a confusing sort of scuffle as if several people were trying to communicate at once, then a male voice seemed to elbow the others out of the way.

'I was killed,' he said gruffly. 'I was killed here.'

Now we were getting somewhere, I thought with satisfaction.

155

'Here?' I said. 'What happened?'

Immediately I felt a rushing, falling sensation as if I was falling through the air and my neck and head hurt badly.

'I went right down the stairs,' said the man. 'From top to bottom. That's what did it.'

'Which stairs, dear?' I asked, because we'd just walked round every inch of the restaurant and hadn't come across a flight of stairs.

The man sighed as if I was being unusually dense. 'I'll show you,' he said.

Immediately in my mind I was standing at the top of a flight of steep, narrow stairs with an arch over them. They descended down somewhere gloomy and would need artificial light over them all the time. They were so steep that I could well believe it was dangerous to fall down them.

'I see what you mean,' I told the man. 'But are you sure the stairs are here? I haven't seen any.'

'Of course they're here. Right in this building,' he insisted.

I turned to Richard and Barbara. 'Can you think what he means?'

They exchanged glances. 'Well,' said Richard, 'there's a bar under the restaurant. It's nothing to do with us but it's in the same building and it has its own separate entrance down a flight of stairs just like the ones you described.'

'Do you know if anyone has fallen down them and been killed?' I asked.

He shook his head.

'Well, see if you can find out. I'm sure there has and I'm sure it was a man.'

Having no love link to work from made talking to the man very difficult because he had no special desire to talk to Richard or Barbara and as soon as he grew bored he wandered away. Nevertheless we persevered. He mentioned quite a few names. Some of them meant something to the Possners, most didn't. Then he said Derek, or Eric.

Richard shook his head.

'They don't know him, dear,' I said. But shortly afterwards, as if he felt they really did know, he said, 'In connection with Derek – Bentley.'

Again the Possners couldn't place it. Neither Derek nor Bentley meant a thing to them.

But the vibrations were getting muddled again and I thought I heard another voice come in.

'I was killed, you know,' he said.

'Yes I know, you told me,' I replied, thinking I'd made a mistake and the first man was still talking.

'No, I didn't. This is Billy,' he said loudly. 'I was killed and it wasn't an accident.'

As he spoke I had a brief picture of a young man with flaming ginger hair standing behind Barbara's chair and there was a strong sweaty smell of gymnasiums.

'I was a waiter, you know,' he said, 'and I was killed.'

'This place didn't used to be a gym, did it, or have anything to do with gyms or boxing?' I asked.

'Not as far as we know,' said Richard, 'but we've only been here six months and I don't think the people before us stayed very long. There's no knowing what it was ten or twenty years ago.'

But then the first man was back with more names. They meant nothing to the Possners and I could see Richard looking at his watch. It was time to bring the sitting to a close.

'Now about these things that have been happening,' I said to whoever was listening. 'It's got to stop. You're worrying these young people and it's not fair.'

There was more scuffling then a voice said, 'Didn't mean to do any harm . . . sorry,' and faded away.

'Well, I don't think you'll have any more trouble,' I told Barbara and Richard. 'He says he's sorry.'

They seemed quite happy and we gathered up our things ready to leave as the first customers came through the door.

'Oh, before you go, Doris, would you like to see the staircase you mentioned?' asked Barbara.

I said I would. She led me out into the street and there next to the restaurant was another door. Barbara tried it but it was locked.

'Oh, what a shame,' she said, 'the stairs are behind that door. They're terribly steep.'

I stared at it for a moment or two.

'Would they finish at a point just below your bar?'

'Yes, I suppose they would.'

Immediately I thought of the cold spot I'd felt when I stood behind the bar, the one I'd blamed on the ice bucket. Also the fact that Val had heard her voice when she was probably standing near the same place. I was just about to mention this to Barbara when a band of writing over the top of the door caught my eye. It was the details of the licensee of the bar and his name was written up there, small but clear. Mr Derek Bentley.

'That's the Derek!' I cried in triumph.

Excitedly Barbara came to see and she called Richard. Derek Bentley, as plain as plain, the name that had come through during the sitting.

'I'll be right back,' said Richard. 'There's someone I can ask.' And he darted off up the road.

'Some of the people round here have been in the area several years,' Barbara explained.

Minutes later Richard was back, a big grin all over his face.

'Derek Bentley is dead,' he said. 'He died one night after falling down those stairs.'

Well, that seemed to settle it. John and I headed back to Fulham pleased with the afternoon's work.

But as it turned out, that wasn't the end of the story. Weeks later we heard that though the name calling and trouble with clocks had stopped the mechanical problems were still going on.

Lights kept switching on and off. The stereo kept breaking down, a blade mysteriously flew off a machine landing only inches away from the chef and within an hour of laughing and joking about the ghostly Billy, three of the boys who helped in the restaurant all suffered minor but unpleasant accidents.

This puzzled me until I remembered that if the cold spot behind the bar hadn't been caused by the ice, then there were two cold spots in the restaurant. This would explain why I'd contacted two different men, Derek Bentley and the mysterious Billy. At the end of the sitting when I'd asked them to stop messing about only one voice had agreed and sent its apologies. Looking back I think that voice must have belonged to Derek Bentley. Billy refused to commit himself and it seems Billy is still making his presence felt.

So who is Billy? At the moment we don't know. Richard and Barbara haven't yet found anyone who's lived in the area long enough to give them a clue.

I can see that one of these days I'll have to go along and have another word with Billy.

Around this time I seemed to go into a phase of spontaneously seeing spirit adults. I can't think why this should be unless it's doing so much work with children that's caused it. Maybe because I always see spirit children and I've seen so many of them lately, my psychic eye is getting so highly tuned that it's picking out spirits all over the place.

What with the monk and the flame-haired Billy at the restaurant in Swallow Street I felt sure I'd seen my quota of adults for the year. It's been a long time since my days as a young medium when I was so full of undisciplined psychic energy that I was seeing things all over the place and our homes were full of knocks and bangs and objects flying about. Yet suddenly here it was starting to happen all over again.

I was still rather run down after my operation and was wondering how I was going to get through the string of engagements looming ahead, when Lee Everett offered to give me some healing. Now John is a healer and he was already treating me himself, but I've always believed that every little helps and I accepted gratefully.

As usual Lee arrived with a companion. Not Annie this time but her sister.

'I hope you don't mind,' she said.

'Not a bit.'

I led them into the living-room and Lee's sister and I sat down on the sofa, while Lee sat opposite by the window. We were chatting away and Lee brought me up to date with the latest news, when a sudden movement caught my eye. I glanced up to see a man had appeared in the room.

My sofa is a three-seater. I was sitting at one end and Lee's sister sat at the other. To my amazement the man crossed the room and plonked himself down on the vacant seat between us. My eyes widened . . . I glanced quickly at the other two but they didn't seem to have noticed anything unusual. Lee was in mid-sentence and her sister was listening attentively. So, too, was our unannounced guest.

He wasn't doing any harm so I decided to leave him be.

If he wanted to drop in to listen to a bit of conversation I couldn't blame him. He looked so real and solid he had probably not been over long. Perhaps he missed our company.

'Well, I suppose I'd better start the healing, Doris,' said Lee suddenly. 'Change places with me, Bren.'

Obediently Brenda stood up but as she did so the man laid his hand on her knee.

'Don't go, Bren,' he said sadly.

But of course Brenda couldn't hear him or see him. He failed to stop her and, as she stood, his hand went right through her knee. The man disappeared.

Yet the sadness in his voice touched me. The man hadn't dropped in for a chat. He belonged to Brenda and he wanted to see her. Therefore I felt I must say something.

'Look, Brenda, I don't know what to do about this,' I said slowly, 'but it's so definite I must tell you. There's a man been sitting between us and as you got up to go he said, "Don't go, Bren."'

One look at her face told me I was right to mention it.

'Oh dear, it's your husband, isn't it?' I added.

She nodded, her eyes full of tears. 'He only passed last Friday,' she whispered.

Well, what could I do? After the healing session Brenda and I had a sitting and her husband was able to return with messages of love and reassurance.

Shortly after this there was a small gap in my diary and since the weather was fine, John suggested it would be a good idea if we went down to our caravan for a few days.

For a long time we've been dreaming about moving out of London. John would like to have a garden to potter in and I must admit it would be nice to live somewhere where you could hear the birds singing and when you walked out of your front door you breathed lungfuls of fresh air instead of traffic fumes.

We've finally had to face the fact that it would never happen. I need to be in a central position for my work, or people wouldn't be able to find me, and we can't afford anything else in such an area. It looked as if we would have to give up our dreams for ever. Then someone told us about caravans. Apparently you could buy them on country sites complete with furniture and some of them even had little garden plots attached. It sounded ideal for us.

'We could do with a bolt hole,' said John. 'This place drives you mad at times with the phone going non-stop.'

He was right. Often the phone rang all day and although we don't give out our full address people find us and come to the door on spec. It would be marvellous to have somewhere quiet to escape to now and again, where we could rest well away from the pleading eyes which were so difficult to refuse.

Terry was just as enthusiastic about the idea, and he kept bringing us advertisements of suitable places. Eventually we picked out a place in the middle of nowhere about an hour's drive from the flat.

Terry took us down to see it one weekend and we were all thrilled with it. It was in a small, green park surrounded by fields and it had two bedrooms, a bathroom, kitchen, living-room and a little garden. When you stood still and listened you could hear nothing, nothing but silence and birdsong.

'Oh, John,' I sighed, 'I don't care if we go bankrupt. Let's have it.'

So we did.

Soon John was pottering happily in the garden, I could sit out in a deckchair and watch him when the weather was fine and Terry was making lots of new friends. We all enjoyed it for different reasons.

Down in the country I tried not to think about my work at all so I was very surprised when I walked into our sitting-room one morning to find a strange lady sitting in the chair by the window, waving through the glass at the passers-by.

For a moment I wondered if I could have wandered into the wrong caravan by mistake, it was still so new to us. Then I realized that it was our chair she was sitting in and those were our flowers in the vase on the table.

Maybe she was one of our new neighbours. I took a step closer and she heard me. She turned and gave me a lovely smile.

'Hello, dear,' she said as if she'd known me all her life.

'Hello, dear,' I replied and then I blinked. She disappeared like a puff of smoke.

Even though I'm used to such things it's always a surprise when it happens because spirit people look so real. Often they look no different, no less solid than the people you pass in the street. I don't know where this idea of ghostly beings drifting about in long white sheets comes from but it's certainly not inspired by real contact with the spirit people.

'D'you think she could have had the van before us?' I asked John later when I'd explained what happened.

'Probably,' he said, 'but the neighbours are bound to know. We can ask them.'

'We'll be careful how we put it though, John. They don't know us from Adam and if we start saying there's a ghost in our caravan they'll think we're crackers!'

John laughed but he took the point. We made our enquiries as discreetly as we could, but even so it was rather difficult to get the phrasing right.

'You wouldn't know if a lady ever passed over in this van?' I asked our neighbour soon afterwards.

He nearly choked on his tea.

'What makes you say that? I've been here two years and I've not heard of anyone dying.'

I'd obviously not handled the subject very well.

'Oh I just wondered that's all – about who had the van before us, I mean.'

'Oh, I can tell you that,' he said and launched in to a description of the previous owners who were very much alive and kicking.

Nothing more was said and it seemed as if the identity of our elderly visitor would remain a mystery.

Then on another visit a few weeks later we met the people whose garden backed on to ours. They had been away on holiday when we were last down so we'd not had a chance to talk to them. We soon put that to right. Not long after we arrived we were chatting over the fence like old friends.

'Of course, old Mrs So and So died in the bedroom there,' said the woman suddenly.

I was instantly alert. 'You mean in our van?'

'Oh yes,' she said.

'Tell me, did she used to sit by the lounge window waving to people?'

The woman stared at me in amazement. 'Why, how did you know? She was in a wheelchair and she used to wave to me when I took the dog for a walk.'

So that was it. The van used to belong to her and she'd come back to have a look at us and see that we were taking care of it.

Incidentally, if anyone who has read my last two books wonders what we did with our cat, Matey, while we made our jaunts down to the van, I have to explain that we didn't leave him behind and we wouldn't have dreamed

164

of leaving him behind. Sadly, he passed over before we got our country retreat, which is a shame because he would have loved the garden.

One day he simply disappeared. He didn't come in for his meal as he normally did and when he hadn't turned up by nightfall I was fearing the worst.

'He's probably got shut in somewhere,' people suggested to cheer me up. Or, 'It's spring. He's probably having a last fling on the tiles.'

But the next day there was still no sign of him. John and I searched the walkways and the courtyard around the flats and found nothing. Matey seemed to have vanished into thin air.

That afternoon I felt terribly tired.

'I think I'll have a lay down, John,' I said yawning and, unusually for me, I was asleep in minutes. But it wasn't a restful sleep. Dreams came almost at once and in my dreams I saw a very tall man holding the body of a ginger cat in his arms. I couldn't see the man's face but the cat was Matey and I'm pretty sure the man was my father.

When I woke up I knew I'd seen the truth.

'We can put away Matey's bowls,' I told John. 'He won't be coming back. My father's taken him. He's on the other side now.'

We never saw him again.

It's sad because Matey missed his garden when we moved to London and he would have enjoyed stalking about in our little plot at the van. On the other hand I know he's got all the space he wants on the other side, because animals live on just as humans do and we shall see our pets again one day.

It wasn't many weeks before we discovered that even deep in the country we couldn't escape entirely. Word got round in that mysterious way it has and some people were arriving unannounced. I discovered too that, even in the country, I wasn't to escape the lessons Ramanov wanted to teach me.

One evening I was watching television and John had gone round to our neighbour to take back a clothesline we'd borrowed, when I heard a commotion outside. I lifted up the corner of the curtains and saw a lady, a man and two youngsters all coming down the lawn.

'Perhaps they think the place is still for sale,' I thought. Oh well, they'd soon realize their mistake. I went back to my programme.

A few minutes later John came back.

'Hey, love!' he said putting his head round the door. 'There's a lady outside and she doesn't want to bother you but she wondered if she could have a look at you just to make sure it was you.'

'What d'you mean, make sure it's me?' I asked.

'Well somebody told her you were staying down here and she said she wouldn't believe it unless she saw it for herself. She says she doesn't want to be a nuisance, but could she just look at you for a moment.'

Well, what could I do? It was vain but I couldn't resist it. Up I got and out I went onto the verandah and, despite the fact that I was wearing an old sun dress, slippers and no stockings, I stood there feeling like the Queen. My admirers gathered round to gaze at me in awe and I have to admit it was very flattering.

I enjoyed myself thoroughly and granted them much longer than a minute or two. And what was the result of my vanity?

As I stood there on the verandah holding court like the Queen, a mosquito bit me three times.

The next day the bites swelled into hot red lumps that

kept me itching and scratching for days. And as I rubbed away at the blazing skin I couldn't help smiling.

Well, that'll teach you, Doris, I said to myself. What does Ramanov say? 'Your gift is for helping others not for your own self-aggrandisement.'

That's what comes of being vain!

# CHAPTER 10

'Rawlinson,' said a voice.

Startled, I looked up to see who had spoken but even as I did so I realized my mistake. Despite the fact that I wasn't tuned in, it was a spirit voice I was hearing.

'Rawlinson,' it said again. 'Rawlinson.'

The car was speeding along the motorway, engine roaring, tyres loud on the tarmac, yet above the noise I could hear the quiet voice quite distinctly.

I was on my way to a public demonstration in Maidenhead and, as the Berkshire countryside flashed past the window, the name was repeated again and again. It was quite obvious to me that Rawlinson, whoever he or she may be, was going to be important at the coming meeting.

All right, I told the voice in the end, I understand. I'll see what I can do when I get there. I've sometimes wondered in the past how much comfort people can get from mass meetings. I know they are very useful in awakening interest and getting people to ask themselves questions that might never have occurred to them before but can you give much help to individuals? Is it better to give a lot of people a little or a few people a lot? In Maidenhead I got my answer, with the Rawlinson case.

As with all the answers I get in one form or another from Ramanov it was vaguely disconcerting. I was to stop bothering about things I didn't understand, do my job and leave the rest to the spirit world. How much or how little help I thought I was able to give was irrelevant because my messages weren't an end in themselves, but just another link in the chain the spirit world was building.

As far as I was concerned, I wasn't able to give the

Rawlinsons much time, but the spirit world was already at work with them and the information they got from me, on top of the things that had already happened, was all part of a process that was to change their lives.

When I went on stage at Maidenhead I chatted to the audience for a few minutes and told one or two jokes to help them relax. Then as the laughter died away and I could feel a general loosening up all round, I reckoned it was time to start work.

'Now, before I begin,' I said, 'is there anyone here by the name of Rawlinson or who knows anyone called Rawlinson? I've been hearing the name all the way down here so I know it's important.'

There was a stunned silence for a moment, then a man raised his hand.

'I'm Rawlinson.'

Immediately the voice came back, a young man's voice eager to communicate and clearly delighted to have got through first. The names tumbled from him so fast it was difficult to keep up.

'He's talking about someone called Margaret.'

'That's my wife,' said Mr Rawlinson.

'And Joe, or is it John?'

'My daughter's called Joanne.'

'Then there's Paul,' I continued. Then I stopped. The man nodded, yes he knew Paul, but he was clearly very upset. The young man came close in and I realized there was a great tragedy here. He was only nineteen, he said, and there'd been a car crash. In the background other voices were clamouring to be heard. I didn't want to start the evening on too sad a note and I didn't want to embarrass Mr Rawlinson.

'I'll have to move on, I'm afraid,' I told him. 'They're all trying to get through, but don't worry. I'll come back to you.'

As it turned out though, I didn't. There were so many spirit people determined to talk to their friends and relatives in the audience that our time ran out before I was able to return to Mr Rawlinson.

Wearily I left the stage and headed for the kitchen where my customary cup of tea was waiting. I felt rather bad about Mr Rawlinson but I have to go where the spirit voices lead me and that night his son, for I was sure it was his son, had not led me back to his father.

What I hadn't realized, of course, was that Glen, as I later discovered his name to be, was doing it the other way round. He was leading his father back to me.

I was deep into my second cup when suddenly the kitchen door opened and there stood Mr Rawlinson. He hesitated in the doorway obviously unwilling to disturb me.

'It's Mr Rawlinson, isn't it?' I said, motioning him to come in. 'I'm sorry I didn't come back to you but it was too sad. Your son tells me he was only nineteen and he was in an accident. He was coming round a bend, he says, and there was a head-on collision. Two people went over and three ended up in hospital.'

Mr Rawlinson look dumbfounded. 'Yes, that's right. My son and the other driver were killed and three passengers were taken to hospital.'

Glen was back now, loud and clear. 'I was killed instantly,' he said. 'I didn't suffer but I'm so sorry it happened. I shouldn't even have been there. I wouldn't have been there if it hadn't been for Kevin.'

Mr Rawlinson nodded. 'Yes, he was giving Kevin a lift home to Cookham.'

'I'm so sorry for the upset I caused just when I was doing what Dad wanted me to do,' Glen went on. 'Now they're shattered, especially Mum, because I didn't say goodbye.'

'Yes, that's what upset her the most,' said Mr Rawlinson. 'He always said goodbye when he went out but that night she was upstairs and for some reason he didn't call out to her.'

Glen was worried about his mum. 'She's falling apart and she's got to stop because I'm all right. I'm alive and I'm happy. Oh, and tell her Margaret, called Maggie, is looking after me.'

This was gratifying because apparently one of the things that most worried Mrs Rawlinson was that if there was an after life, Glen would be alone because very few of his relatives had gone over. The only one was his grandmother, Margaret, nicknamed Maggie.

On a lighter note Glen added, 'Tell Mum there's lots of sunshine here because she is a great sun fanatic, and tell her that I spend a lot of time in the halls of music. Not just with pop music, good music too.'

Mr Rawlinson drew in his breath. He recognized the phrase. 'In his spare time Glen was a DJ,' he said, 'and he always said, "I don't just play pop music, you know. I play good music." '

Glen went on to give more family names, then he returned to the accident. 'I wouldn't have minded,' he said, 'but I'd only sold a house that morning.'

Apparently Glen was an estate agent and the day of the accident he was particularly happy and excited because he'd just sold his boss's house and he was going on holiday to the South of France the following weekend.

That was about all I was able to do that night and it seemed little enough to me. I was particularly sorry that Eric Rawlinson's wife Margaret wasn't there. Apparently, Glen had only passed a month before and the grief was so strong she felt she couldn't face a public meeting.

What I didn't realize was that the whole family was to

171

experience a real change and a new world was opening up to them quite literally.

My communication, while not much in itself, fitted neatly into what they were finding out, and was further confirmation of the truth.

Several months later Eric and Margaret explained what happened.

'Glen was something special,' said Eric, a property developer and insurance broker. 'He was a positive, lively young man who was great with people. So many people loved him. In fact afterwards, when we were looking through the old photographs, it was difficult to find a picture where Glen didn't have his arm round someone.

'It was impossible to have an argument with him because he always apologized and put his arm round you. He gave out so much love. We're still finding out about the things he did for people and at the hospital where he was a DJ in his spare time, they are putting up a plaque in his memory because they were so fond of him.

'After his death the family were devastated. He was such an extrovert that there was a great void in our lives. Even today nothing can fill it.

'Yet some incredible things have happened. Four days after his death I had the most incredible spiritual experience. I've never known anything like it in my life. It is very difficult to put into words. All I can say is that on Thursday afternoon after the accident I was sitting in the kitchen in a terrible state. I was so distraught, so unhappy.

'Then suddenly the kitchen started to fill with light, a tremendous light like coming out of the fog into bright sunshine and I heard Glen's voice say, "You have to die to be born."

'All at once everything fell into place. Life, death, everything. I knew. I understood. Yet if you ask me what I knew, I couldn't tell you. At the time I felt uplifted, tremendously elated. I've never been so happy in my life. I wanted to rush out and open bottles of champagne.

'I turned to Margaret and she said, "Yes, I know. It happened to me last night." But when I mentioned it to a friend later, thinking he'd understand, he thought I was going out of my mind.

'I wasn't. I've never been saner. I'd seen the truth. Suddenly I understood what all those old clichés like "seen the light" really meant. The elation didn't last. The next day I was depressed again, but the truth remained.

'I don't believe any more. I know.'

The experience caused Eric to read as much as he could on spiritualism and philosophy and everything he read seemed to confirm his feelings. Although he'd never read these subjects before, he instantly recognized what they said. Even the philosophy was familiar.

In the past he'd been a forceful, down-to-earth businessman with little time for such matters. He didn't even know that the spiritualist church existed. Yet when the family came back from a holiday Eric had taken them on to get over the shock of the accident, he found two tickets for the meeting at Maidenhead waiting for him.

'A neighbour got them for me,' he said. 'She had read *Voices in My Ear* and *More Voices* and she thought that seeing Doris might help. There was never any question in my mind that I shouldn't go. I knew I had to go and I knew Glen would contact me. When Doris called out my name I was shocked but somehow not surprised, if you see what I mean.'

Of course, as I found, and as every parent I've ever spoken to has found, Eric discovered that you never get over the loss of a child, but you do learn to live with it. He also realized that it helped to talk about it, and the more he talked the more he became aware of a dimension he'd never noticed before when he was deep in his money-making schemes.

'People are embarrassed to talk about their beliefs,' he said, 'but once you make it clear that you understand, they come out with the most amazing stories. I've discovered that about sixty or seventy per cent of the people I've spoken to are spiritually motivated.

'One man I've known for years wasn't at all surprised by my experiences. "I know you're right," he said, "because of what happened to my brother."

'Apparently his brother had been extremely fond of their grandfather, but while he was away in the Navy, the grandfather died. When the brother's ship docked, the whole family went to meet him and once the greetings were over their mother said, "I'm afraid there's some sad news as well."

' "If it's about Grandad, I know," said the brother. "I know he's gone. He came to me on board and told me."

'The family were astonished but the brother stuck to his story. "He appeared to me on the ship and said goodbye," he said.

'The strange thing is,' Eric added, 'I've heard dozens of stories like that ever since.'

Margaret Rawlinson knows exactly what he means. Although she didn't feel able to attend the Maidenhead meeting, she, too, was learning and discovering.

'That meeting was too soon for me,' she said. 'I was still in the depths of grief. Yet I'm glad Eric went because the things he was able to tell us afterwards helped the whole family so much. We knew nothing about the subject at all. We were feeling terrible, then suddenly there was this joyous news. It brought us such comfort to know that the person we loved was still there and that we'd meet again one day.

'We've been reading books ever since and talking to

people and we have been told the most amazing things. One woman from the village told me that she knew there was life after death because she'd been to the other side. She had been involved in a terrible accident and she had "died" for several minutes. She says she can remember what happened in great detail. She said she was in a tunnel and there was a bright light at the end and she could see all these loving people waiting for her. She was moving along the tunnel towards them and she knew that once she reached the light she would be "over". Then suddenly she was pulled back again and the doctors revived her.

'She also believes she has visited her grandmother – in a dream that she is convinced wasn't a dream. She was very sad because her grandmother died and she hadn't said goodbye. One night she "dreamed" she met her grandmother in a beautiful place. Her grandmother was looking much younger than she remembered her and they hugged and kissed and said goodbye. Most people would say it was a dream, but this woman is quite convinced it actually happened.'

For Eric Rawlinson the tragedy has had far-reaching effects.

'The most important thing that has happened to me since the accident is that I'm no longer afraid of dying. I used to be terribly afraid. I used to wake up in the night in a cold sweat imagining black eternity and vast, endless space. For years I'd been living in terror of death. Now I don't fear it at all. Quite the opposite. I know that death is simply rebirth on a higher level, to a world of beauty and love.

'But it isn't something you can get over to other people. Before all this happened, if you had told me this I wouldn't have believed it. I wouldn't have listened. You can't tell people. It's something they have to experience for themselves. Because of what's happened to me, I know.'

What's more, the experience has made Eric question his values and way of life. He is a successful businessman with a talent for raising money and now he would like to use his talent to help other people.

'I suddenly realized that in his short life, my son had achieved more than I have done in the whole of mine,' he said. 'Now I would like to do something worthwhile for others. In fact, I know I will. When the time is right it will all fall into place and I will see what I have to do.'

After talking to the Rawlinsons I will never again doubt the place that my little snippets of information have in the overall scheme of things and I have been going to public demonstrations with new enthusiasm ever since.

I'm often invited to speak at the Spiritualist Association of Great Britain's headquarters in Belgrave Square, and the last time I was there I had some very vivid communications. At one point I glanced up and saw a little girl dancing round the feet of a woman in the audience. It was quite clear from the way she moved and the way no one took any notice of her that she was a spirit child.

'My name's Helen,' she told me, giggling. 'And this is my mummy.'

Then she skipped up to the platform and got hold of the necklace I was wearing.

'Look round Mummy's neck. Look round Mummy's neck,' she instructed excitedly.

But I was too far away to see her mother's neck or what she was wearing. Helen wasn't going to give up though. After the meeting she accompanied her mother to the front to see me and round her mother's neck I noticed a chain from which hung a tiny picture of Helen.

During the same meeting two young people, a boy and

176

a girl, came to say hello. They were called John and Lorraine, and John's mother was in the audience.

'What happened, love?' I asked John and in reply he gave me what I took to be two contradictory sensations. I could smell gas very strongly but I was also surrounded by water, lots of water. That confused me. Were they gassed or drowned, or was one gassed and the other drowned?

John's mother explained. 'They were on a boat, Doris, and one of the gas bottles was leaking.'

'I tried to get help,' said John, 'but I couldn't make it. I collapsed. It's a good thing Mum didn't look at me afterwards. We were strawberry coloured.'

It was horrifying, of course, yet these two lovely young people were still together and happy.

You hear so many tragic stories on these occasions yet, strangely enough, there is usually a lot of laughter as well. I remember when I gave a similar demonstration shortly afterwards in Hitchin, Hertfordshire, one lady was astonished when I was able to tell her she'd got £42·50 tucked away in a tea caddy. The audience rocked and her face was a picture.

'Yes, I have,' she gasped. '£42·50 exactly!' And she stared at me with great suspicion as if she thought I'd been peeping through the window.

When I was working with a live audience on the Granada television show, *An Evening With Doris Stokes*, we hardly stopped laughing all night. An elderly man with a walking-stick came along to talk to one lady and I could hear his stick tap-tap-tapping in the background.

'He used to use a stick, didn't he?' I said. 'For walking and getting in and out of chairs.'

'Not just for that, either,' she replied tartly. 'He used to whack things with it as well.'

Everyone laughed but the man who had a strong Yorkshire accent wasn't put off.

'When's she going to get rid of that blue hat that's been standing on the wardrobe all these years?' he said. 'She gets it out and puts it back. Why doesn't she throw it away?'

'He's right,' the woman chuckled. 'It's still in its C&A hat bag.'

Then there was the dear old lady who had relatives halfway across the world.

'You've got relatives in Australia, in Melbourne, and relatives in Christchurch, New Zealand,' I told her.

'Yes I have,' she agreed happily.

'And next year they're all coming over to see you for a special celebration.'

'Are they?'

At this there was an irritated hissing in my ear.

'It's a surprise. A surprise,' said a voice. 'You weren't supposed to tell her.'

'Oh dear, I wasn't supposed to say that,' I apologized. 'It's a surprise.'

'It's all right,' the old lady beamed. 'I didn't hear a word.'

The animals got a look-in as well. A little later in the middle of something serious I had to break off and turn to someone else.

'There's a dog called Barney just turned up,' I said to a lady with tight dark curls. 'Do you know Barney?'

'Barney? Why, yes, I do,' she said in surprise. The last contact she'd expected was from her dog.

That was all for the time being, but a few minutes later I was dragged back to her. Oh no, I thought, when I heard what the voice wanted me to tell her. That sounds ridiculous. But the voice insisted.

'All right,' I said in defeat. 'Well, you know Barney,

well, with Barney was there a parrot? They're saying something about a parrot and Barney.'

A great hoot of laughter filled the studio and even the woman giggled.

'A stuffed parrot, yes,' she said. 'Over Barney's basket.'

There were sad cases as well, of course. There was a little boy no more than four or five running up and down the aisle. His name was Anthony he said and he had leukaemia. His parents weren't in the audience but a friend of theirs was. Anthony wanted his parents to know that he was all right now and his hair had grown back.

Then there was the baby girl who was a cot death victim. She'd gone over leaving behind her identical twin, Collette, and the seven-year-old girl whose mother had put a rose and a teddy bear into the coffin with her. Even Barney's owner was there for a more pressing reason than contact with Barney. She had been waiting for twenty-one years for news of her daughter who had never recovered from an operation to repair a hole in her heart.

There were warnings too. One woman was told of her relative's great concern over the cellar steps.

'He's very worried about these steps,' I said. 'Something about a door at the top and a child falling down. He wants you to put a bolt on the door as soon as possible.'

Another woman, there with her young daughter, was warned of a motor-bike.

'There's something about a motor-bike,' I said. 'There's a boy here who was killed on a motor-bike.'

The woman shook her head. 'No, I don't know anyone.'

'No, it's something to do with your daughter. Do you know anyone who was killed on a bike?'

She said she didn't.

If I hadn't been so certain this message was meant for them I would have thought I'd got the wrong contacts. As it was I knew it fitted in somehow.

'Who wants a motor-bike?' I asked.

'I do,' said the daughter.

'She's always on about it,' said her mother.

That was it. No, they were saying emphatically on the other side. No, and they pointed to the boy who had been killed.

'No way,' I said. 'She mustn't get a bike. They've brought this boy back as a warning of what could happen. She mustn't have a bike.'

The girl looked distinctly fed up as if she wished she had stayed at home.

'I shan't be allowed to have one now,' she muttered gloomily.

I felt a bit sorry for her but I wouldn't take back what I'd said. I've seen the parents of so many children who've lost their lives on motor-cycles.

Last year I was also invited to appear on the *Russell Harty Show*. Russell was a lovely boy but he seemed a bit nervous at first and he tried to rush me round to too many people in the audience.

That's the trouble with television. Producers don't like it if you stay too long with one person or if the messages are not evenly distributed round the audience. I can see their point but unfortunately I have to go where the voices take me and I can't force or hurry them.

I was a bit disappointed with my work that night for this reason. I didn't feel I had time to establish a rapport with the audience before Russell was rushing me again.

'Now,' he said, 'we have a surprise mystery guest here tonight. We thought it would be a bit of fun if Doris could discover her identity.'

Well, I was certainly surprised. I'm a medium not a mind reader, after all, but I hate to refuse a challenge.

'I can't promise anything,' I said slowly, 'but I'll have a go.'

The mystery woman was sitting in another room speaking to the studio by telephone. We only had a couple of minutes but soon I was listening to a warm Irish voice.

I've been to Ireland a couple of times and the accent sounded identical to me to the accents I'd heard on my travels, yet something made me wary.

'It's not genuine,' Ramanov whispered. 'Be careful.'

'I don't think this lady usually speaks with an Irish accent,' I said slowly. But, even as I was talking, spirit voices were drawing close, hoping for contact with her. One of them muttered something about the stage.

'I think this lady is something to do with the stage,' I said.

Then I heard the name Minnie.

The mystery woman said she knew someone of this name.

Next came the name Pat.

'And I'm getting the name Pat. Do you know anyone called Pat?'

There was a tiny pause as if she had taken a deep breath before answering.

'Yes, I know a Pat,' she admitted.

I began to relax. The contact was there. It would be all right.

'Well, I'm sorry, Doris,' said Russell Harty, so suddenly I jumped, 'but that's all we've got time for. And now here is our mystery guest.'

I was brought so swiftly back down to earth my mind was spinning and before I fully realized what was happening, the actress, Pat Phoenix, was walking towards me. I was thrilled. Pat was one of my favourite characters from *Coronation Street* and I never missed an episode if I could help it.

'Hello, Doris,' she said, smiling in such a friendly way

181

I felt as if I'd known her for years. But then I suppose in a way I had. She'd been coming into my living room twice a week for as long as I could remember.

'You know, if you'd have had more time you would have got me,' she said. 'You were getting so close.'

She was just as nice and natural as I'd always imagined and we became friends. To this day Pat regularly phones to see how I am and she gave me an autographed copy of her book which has pride of place in my bookcase.

Yes, my work does take me all over the place and into some very unlikely situations, from large halls to television studios and radio phone-ins, as well, of course, as my own living-room which has to double as a 'sitting' room, since it's our only reception room. When I'm working, poor John and Terry are banished to the kitchen!

Perhaps one of the loveliest aspects of my work is when I'm asked to be the medium at a naming service. This is the spiritualist version of a baptism, I suppose, but we don't baptize our children with water, because water is supposed to wash away sin. We believe that every newborn child is pure. They come straight from God or the spirit world and therefore they know no sin.

We name them with white flowers as a symbol of their purity. The other unusual feature of this service is that the child receives two names. The name his parents have chosen for him and his spirit name. This is the name he was last known by in the spirit world before he was born. To find out this name, a medium has to be present to tune in and ask.

This service isn't only for children, adults can take part too and I was 'named' myself in a lovely ceremony on the Isle of Man. It is not essential but I thought it would be a nice thing to do, a sort of public affirmation of my faith. The medium told me my spirit name was Lena, and John was given the name Samuel. Quite a coincidence that, since my father, who still helps me, was called Sam.

I took part in a very moving but informal naming just a few weeks ago, but it came about most unexpectedly. We have known Del Robinson, president of the Wimbledon Church, for years. When we came back from Australia last time it was Del who arranged a wonderful welcome home party for us. So naturally we were very excited for him when he told us he was about to become a grandfather for the first time.

The event was very close when Del's partner, Reg, happened to be visiting us. We were changing our car and he had brought the new one down to us. Anyway we were standing in the kitchen having a cup of tea when he asked if he could make a phone call.

'Jackie's been taken into hospital today, you see,' he said, 'and I wondered if there was any news.'

'Help yourself, love,' I said. 'You know where the phone is.'

He turned and went out into the hall but before he reached the phone, Rose, Del's mother, came bustling through.

'He needn't bother,' she said proudly. 'I can tell you. It's a fine big boy. A *big* boy. It's here. He's been born,' and I thought she said they were going to call him Alec.

'Reg,' I called, 'phone by all means, but Rose has just told me the baby's here and it's a fine big boy.'

A startled look crossed Reg's face as if he didn't know whether to believe me or not.

'Well, I'll just check, if it's all the same to you,' he said with a sheepish grin.

I laughed and went back into the kitchen as he began to dial. It was 1.40 by our kitchen clock.

Reg was connected immediately and his voice floated in from the small hall. We could hear him getting more and more incredulous with every word until John and I had to put our hands over our mouths to stop ourselves from laughing out loud.

'Already . . .' said Reg. 'What? A boy . . . Really? That's a big one . . . and when . . . half past one? You mean ten minutes ago? Well, I'm blowed.'

This went on for some time. Then there was a click and a bemused Reg came back to the kitchen.

'You were right,' he said reaching for his tea. 'It's a boy. Born ten minutes ago and he is a fine big lad too, nine pounds, seven ounces.'

There was just one thing wrong. I thought Rose had said he was going to be called Alec. But he wasn't. It was Ashley.

The story didn't end there. Del Robinson was so delighted he asked us to go to see the baby.

We had a marvellous time. The little flat was full of white flowers and Ashley was the sweetest little fellow you ever saw, with smooth creamy skin, a tiny button nose and a few thistledown tufts of fair hair. I took him in my arms and tuned in.

Rose came over immediately for another look. 'Isn't he lovely? My great grandson,' she sighed.

Then another, firmer, voice took over and I realized I was dealing with someone on a much higher plane. He spoke with kindness and yet there was authority in his voice, too. It was the sort of voice you obeyed instinctively.

'I am the baby's guide. My name is Clear Water,' he said. 'His spirit name is John.' Then he was gone.

I passed this on to the parents and as I spoke I could hear cameras clicking away. The proud grandparents wanted to make sure that every event in Ashley's life was well documented.

184

We moved on to the tea and sandwiches and I kept Ashley on my knee for as long as Jackie would allow.

'Isn't it strange?' I said to Del. 'Ashley's spirit name is the same as my baby's earth name.' And because of this I felt a strong bond with him.

There was another surprise in store. A couple of weeks later the photographs were developed and Del noticed something strange about the picture that was taken as I named Ashley. There was me, quite clearly in the foreground with Ashley in my arms, but up near the ceiling to my left was a large ball of white light and if you looked closely you could make out the face of a baby in it. The light was hovering in front of the dark brown curtains and Del couldn't understand it at all. There was no glass or mirror anywhere near that could have caused a reflection.

He asked the photographer for an explanation but the photographer was equally baffled.

Since then we've shown the picture to many people and without telling them why we ask them what they can see, if anything, in the light. Most of them say without hesitation 'A baby' although some look at it for a long time twisting it this way and that before at last it falls into place.

'Oh yes, I can see it now,' they say. 'It's funny once you've seen it, it jumps out at you and you can't understand why you couldn't see it before.'

What's the explanation? I don't really know. My own guess is that John Michael was present and showed himself in the form that I would best remember him – as a baby, not much bigger than the one I was holding in my arms.

The spirit world loves babies and I often get news of them before the parents know themselves.

When I was working on the Granada programme, I

was talking to one of the men connected with the show and I said, 'You've got two children, haven't you?'

He laughed. 'No, only one, Doris,' he said.

'Well, they're telling me two,' I said. 'If you've only got one at the moment, you're going to have two soon.'

He shrugged it off. Anyone can say that. But a week later his wife told him she was pregnant.

In Australia they were tickled pink because I was able to tell them that the Princess of Wales was pregnant before the official news came out.

It was on 6 October 1981 and some Australian reporters had come to interview me. The royal wedding was still in everyone's minds and they were talking about the young couple.

'When d'you think they'll start a family?' asked the reporters.

'Well,' I started to say, 'I think they'll wait until . . .' but then I stopped. That was just Doris Stokes guessing, but over the top of my opinion came something more substantial from the spirit world.

'No, I don't think,' I corrected myself, 'I know. She's pregnant now.'

As I said it I nearly had kittens, because I don't go round predicting things and I don't profess to be a fortune teller. But this came through so spontaneously I had to say it.

Well, of course, it caused a great stir. The Australian papers splashed the headline all over the place. 'Doris Stokes says Princess Di is Pregnant!' and the Sydney *Sunday Telegraph* reported, 'Mrs Stokes, who predicted the marriage of Prince Charles and Lady Diana Spencer . . . predicts the birth of a Royal babe about July next year.'

It frightened the life out of me. Supposing I was wrong?

Boy, was I relieved when a few weeks later Buckingham Palace released the official news.

And what did the Australian papers do? Across the front pages: 'How Doris Stokes Knew Before the Queen!'

# CHAPTER 11

In the distance I could hear a train coming.

It was dark and cold and the noise was getting louder and louder. Beneath my feet the rails were vibrating, the whole line singing with the approaching train. Suddenly lights filled the night, a blast of air shook my body and my senses were drowned in a terrible roar.

I had a brief glimpse of a motor-bike with a crash helmet placed neatly on the saddle. Then the picture went out as if a bulb had blown.

It is always a tragedy to lose a child but the worst tragedy of all is to lose that child through suicide.

All parents suffer guilt, but the parents of children who have chosen to die face unimaginable torment. For the rest of their lives they will be tortured by endless questions. 'Why?', 'Why did he do it?', 'Why didn't I realize?', 'How could he have been so unhappy without me knowing?', 'Where did I go wrong?', 'Was there something else I could have done?'

The questions never stop because there is no answer.

Other parents can find comfort in the thought that accidents will happen, illness strikes anywhere. But the parents whose children commit suicide have only the knowledge that the life they gave was deliberately thrown away because it became intolerable. Their love just wasn't enough . . .

Or at least that's how it seems to them. If only they could understand that they are not to blame. Neither are the children. The children who do these terrible things are as sick as they would be if they had leukaemia. This is understood on the other side where they are not punished but nursed back to health. And when they are well again these children are horrified at the suffering they have caused.

Nigel Cox was a loving, apparently happy boy who one night stepped in front of a train. When he realized what he'd done he was so distraught he couldn't rest until he received his mother's forgiveness.

In addition to her grief Betty Cox was haunted by an impression of Nigel standing behind her, sobbing. She thought she was going out of her mind. In fact the bond between mother and son was so strong she was simply sharing his anguish.

It was Betty's friend, Lois, who first contacted me. She was afraid for Betty, she explained. Since the tragedy she'd been unable to get over her grief and they were afraid of what she might do. She so loved Nigel that she felt her life was not worth living without him.

It was obvious that Nigel was a special child – well, listen to Betty's description:

'He was a wonderful baby, Doris. He was so contented. He never cried. He grew up to be a happy lad with a great sense of humour. We had a lot of fun together. I miss the laughs. He was very generous even to the point of being taken for granted, but he enjoyed helping others. The last two years he loved to help his friends with their bikes and they loved him so much that over a hundred of them came to his funeral.'

Nigel was there as soon as I tuned in and it was clear his grief was as strong as his mother's. He was sobbing and all I could hear was, 'Forgive me, forgive me.'

Until he heard his mother say the words I couldn't get anything else out of him.

'Of course I forgive you, Nigel,' Betty said at last when she realized the problem. Immediately the atmosphere changed. A weight had been lifted from Nigel's shoulders.

189

'I'm so sorry for what I did,' he told me. 'I must have had a brain storm.'

As we talked, he explained that he had everything to live for. A loving family, lots of friends and the prospect of a good job when he finished college. Then things started to go wrong. One evening he went out on a recently acquired motor-bike and he was stopped by the police. He didn't have an MOT certificate for it and he was very worried that they would take him to court over this.

Had he been his normal self this wouldn't have been an insurmountable problem but he wasn't his normal self. A few weeks before he had been attacked in a disco and he had suffered a broken nose and concussion.

'Everyone thought I had recovered from the attack but I hadn't really,' Nigel told me. 'I changed after that. My personality changed.'

'Yes, he's right,' said Betty, 'he did change. He used to shout a lot over little things which wasn't like him.'

'But Nigel, why did you do it, love?' I asked. 'What happened that night?'

He sighed. 'I don't know why. It was like a brain storm.' Suddenly everything seemed too much for him. That terrible scene at the railway track flashed into my mind. Nigel rode to the railway line. Stood his beloved bike beside the track, placed his crash helmet on the saddle and walked in front of a train.

'Why didn't they do a post mortem on my head?' he cried. 'They would have found a blood clot in my brain. That's what did it.'

But he was all right now, he wanted to assure his mother. The only thing that made him unhappy was her unhappiness. He was being looked after by his grandmother and he often visited his family at their cottage in

Leicestershire. He knew about his sister's wedding and he wanted her to know that he would be there.

By the end of the sitting both Betty and Nigel seemed calmer and afterwards Betty wrote to me:

'Lois and I were on cloud nine coming back from London, so excited by the marvellous contact. Lois said I was looking different, the strain of sadness gone from my eyes. Funny that, for my friends at work today said I looked happier . . .

'Now I feel at peace that Nigel is safe with my mother and all the family. I am content to wait to join him when only a few weeks ago I felt I could not live without him . . .'

Margery Foden-Clarke was in a similar state to Betty when she came to see me. Her son, David, went out to the kitchen one Sunday afternoon to make a cup of tea, or at least that's what he said he was going to do. Instead, he hanged himself.

It seemed so senseless. He was surrounded by loving people, his mother, his sister, his wife and his two beautiful daughters. He had a nice home and a good job. What's more, he was a considerate man. What on earth could have made him bring such distress to his family and horror to his wife who found the body?

It was a question that whirled round Margery's head endlessly. She sat in my living-room fiddling with her tea-cup explaining the things that most bothered her about the tragedy.

'Well, let's see what David has to say,' I said and tuned in.

At once I heard a man's voice, very warm and loving yet there was tension underneath.

'I tried very hard, you know,' he said. 'I tried so hard with my life . . . but there was something at the back of my mind. I thought I had a brain tumour.

191

'I was ill. I wasn't kidding. Sometimes I felt as if my head would burst. I used to hold my head in my hands, but I couldn't make them understand . . .'

Margery agreed that David had been worried about his health but the doctor could find nothing wrong with him.

David went on to give more family names, then he returned to the day of the tragedy.

'I was going out to make some tea and then suddenly it was all too much for me. I said I feel like ending it all, and I thought someone said, "Why don't you?" The pain came back so I took some tablets and I don't remember much more.' That's when he hanged himself.

'I just wanted peace and quiet,' he said, 'and I wanted the pain to stop but it didn't work out like I thought. I was still alive. I went to hospital over here and I slept.'

When he woke again on the other side the pain had gone and he had time to realize what he had done to his family. He seemed happy in the spirit world but he wanted his family to be happy too.

'I wish my wife well,' he said. 'I hope she meets some nice man who will look after my children. Could you ask my mother to go out and do some voluntary work or something? She gets very lonely. She lives alone with just her little dog.'

Like Nigel he was sorry for what he had done.

'Can you forgive me?' he asked his mother. 'I'm afraid I left a lot of chaos behind . . .'

I still see Margery from time to time. She has her bad days, of course, we all do. But she feels close to David. He often makes his presence felt in the house and she knows that whenever she needs him, he's not very far away.

# CHAPTER 12

Edinburgh<br>1 September 1982

Dear Doris Stokes,

Last night my daughter and I went to the Assembly Rooms to see you.

Whilst we were waiting in the queue to get in I said to my daughter, 'If all these spirits are lining up to give messages your father will be saying, After you, After you. He's so bloody polite he'll either be last or miss it altogether.'

Well, I was the last person you spoke to. The one who lost a wallet with £25·00 in it and who has an anniversay coming up this month. And then you said I must finish now. Oh, the frustration of not being able to hear more!

Anyway, my daughter and I were both so thrilled at the little you told us we came away from the town hall feeling so happy.

Is there any chance of a private sitting? I'm keeping my fingers crossed.

Yours very hopefully<br>Mrs Miller

Edinburgh<br>6 September 1982

Dear Mrs Stokes,

Because of the way you coped last night in what must have been very difficult conditions I must thank you and Ramanov.

You got through to me (I was in a blue dress seated on your 'actor's' right) through 'someone in a brewery'. This was my father who died in the 1914 war along with three of my mother's brothers. A whole family of young men slaughtered.

The other name, Duncan, amazed me so I thought immediately of Frank Duncan (you gave me Frank later) but I remembered after I left the hall how when I was very young, Isadora Duncan, the great dancer, was brought through as a guide. You also gave me Louise and as we have French ancestry this is likely.

The two wedding rings was right and the necklace.

I intend returning tonight. I have never had my Dad come through before.

Much love to you
Jean Bruce

Edinburgh
9 September 1982

Dear Doris,

I attended two of your meetings in the Assembly Rooms this month. I have read both your books and look forward to the one you are writing at the moment.

I listened to you speaking to the young woman whose mother had passed on with leukaemia. It was a privileged experience. Then just after that you had us laughing heartily about the couple who had been left to look after a very spoiled pussy cat!

Thank you for coming to Edinburgh.

Yours
Mary Sleight

Strathclyde
10 September 1982

Dear Doris,

I had to write to you. I was the lady whose little girl was there Monday and Tuesday night. Thanks a million, Doris. I was too full to speak much. I would love you to have a photo but I cannot part with the one I have.

I see my little one often. I am one of the fortunate ones who have seen spirit in body.

Oh, Doris, thanks a million. I tried for a reading but I know the ones who were lucky are the people most needing comfort. Please remember my wee one at your Christmas party.

God bless you
Rose Keenan


Dumfries
11 September 1982

Dear Doris,

It was so nice to meet you and you looked much younger than the picture on the books.

I will never meet anyone who could reassure me more that I will meet my darling Morag again. I'm sorry I was so dull and upset. I need the drugs to help me through my days and work.

A lot of the names you gave me meant nothing at the time but afterwards I remembered a lot of them. Derek is Fiona's boyfriend. I wondered what Morag would have said about that.

You will see from Morag's photo that she is just as you described. How I wish the accident never happened and we could all be struggling on together, but at least I know that one day I can put my arms round her again.

I am so grateful that someone like you, Doris, has been given this gift.

God bless you,<br>Moira

One of the most exciting things I did last year was to take part in the Edinburgh Festival and these letters are just a handful, chosen at random from the hundreds I received after my visit.

Now what, you're probably wondering, was I doing at the Edinburgh Festival amongst all that ultra-modern culture and talent? I can only say I often wondered the same thing myself.

The place was full of weird people. Very nice people, as it happened, but definitely weird to a lady of sixty-three like me.

I couldn't understand it at all. Take the frog, for instance. What would you say to a frog who approached you in the restaurant as you were quietly sipping your morning coffee? There I was, just back from the hair-dressers, all nice and relaxed after a soothing spell under the drier and I looked up from my coffee to find a frog standing there. Well, it wasn't a real frog. Underneath, I think there was a young girl but her feet were painted green, her hands were painted green, she was dressed in a brown baggy suit and she was wearing a great papier mâché frog's head over her own.

I think I put my cup down with rather a clank at this extraordinary sight, but the girl didn't seem to notice anything unusual. Making no reference at all to her appearance, she said:

'I just wanted to tell you that I saw your show the other night. I thought it was marvellous. When I saw you sitting here I just had to come over and speak to you.'

'Oh,' I said. 'Well, thank you very much.'

Somehow my eyes remained fixed on this great papier mâché head and I couldn't think of anything else to say.

She smiled, at least I think she did under that mask; if she didn't, her voice certainly smiled, and wished me luck. Then she was off to wherever she'd come from. I looked across at John but for once I was lost for words.

There were many other strange sights that fortnight but gradually we got accustomed to them. When I walked into the foyer and saw two girls dressed from head to foot in black, patiently painting each other's faces with multi-coloured squares, triangles and circles, it hardly even struck me as unusual.

Edinburgh was a beautiful place. The wind was freezing and there were steep, cobbled streets that were a bit difficult at times but one look at that great rugged castle all floodlit on its rock and you forgot the cold. And I must say the bracing air certainly did me good. Despite the fact that I was working hard, I went home without the dark circles under my eyes that had been there for so long I thought they were a permanent feature of my face.

It would be much nicer this time if we stayed in a self-contained flat rather than a hotel, John and I thought. That way we needn't worry about bothering people for meals at odd hours and we could come and go as we pleased. So we asked some friends to find us a flat for the fortnight.

I must say they did us proud. The place they found belonged to a Mr Wong and you could have put our flat in London into the sitting-room and still have had space to spare.

When we walked in for the first time we just dropped

197

our suitcases and gaped. One wall was covered entirely with mirror tiles. Another was orange with curtains to match and on another wall was a full-length picture of Gordon Jackson dressed as the butler from *Upstairs Downstairs*. As for the kitchen, it was so smart and modern I reckoned you'd need a pilot's licence to operate the gadgets. Wouldn't it be lovely if I could take it home with me, I thought.

We were certainly comfortable, the city was beautiful and the atmosphere in the streets was friendly and exciting. Nevertheless, I was apprehensive.

I couldn't see how I fitted into this modern young festival. Surely the sort of people who came to see all this experimental theatre and dance wouldn't be the sort of people who would be interested in a granny like me. Supposing nobody came to the demonstrations? I'd look a proper Charlie then.

Ramanov must have been grinding his teeth in frustration to hear me doubting again. He had always told me to trust. If I would only trust I would have no worries. And, of course, I should have known it would be all right. The spirit world would not have sent me to the festival if they didn't think it was important.

That first night I had to work hard to get a rapport with the audience and then when I did, I seemed to be getting the wrong messages.

A young girl came through. She said her name was Morag and she gave me a Scottish surname as well, but I've been asked not to mention it. She said she was looking for Moira and that she had Robert with her. This information caused a great silence to fall over the audience. Nobody could place a Morag.

'Sorry, love,' I said. 'There's no one here who knows you.'

Reluctantly Morag went away and after that the other messages flowed.

The next night, however, Morag was back. She was a persistent girl. She seemed to think Moira ought to be present, but still no one claimed her and I had to send her away without making a contact. Again the sitting went well after she'd gone.

Soon afterwards, however, a lady who said her name was Moira telephoned me. Someone had told her about the unclaimed message and she thought it might be for her. Her daughter's name was Morag and Morag's father, Robert, was also on the other side. It sounded pretty conclusive to me and she asked if she could have a private sitting.

'All right, love,' I said, flicking through the crammed appointments in my diary. 'Could you manage next Friday at twelve?'

She said she could.

In the meantime the public demonstrations were attracting quite a following. I remember one at 5.00 in the afternoon when the rapport was so good I couldn't seem to stop and the mood changed from happiness to sadness and back again with every message that came through.

A young mother who had gone over at an early age with leukaemia came back to talk to her daughter. She gave several family names and then she said that one of the girl's sisters, Donna I believe it was, was getting married.

'Would you ask her to put one small rosebud in her bouquet for me?' she asked. 'And say "That's mum. Mum'll be there." '

At this the girl suddenly broke down in tears and as I glanced up, pausing to give her a moment to compose herself, I saw that the audience was a forest of handkerchiefs. Even the men were crying.

Five minutes later there was a complete contrast. The spirit light bounced over to two old ladies sitting side by side. They were sisters, alike as two peas, and a voice told me their names and various personal details.

Every time I said something that was right, they dug each other in the ribs, almost knocking each other off their chairs, and they were laughing so much they could hardly speak.

Suddenly whoever was talking from the other side said, 'And tell them we know they've got the big ginger cat and they're having to look after it.'

There was a gasp at this and more tremendous digs. Then they went off into hysterics.

'Is that right?' I asked. 'The cat belongs to your sister and she's gone off to Australia?'

'Yes,' spluttered one of them. 'She has and she's left me the cat to look after and blooming expensive it is, too. She didn't tell me it was on a special diet!'

Well, the place was rocking so much heads kept appearing round the door to see what on earth we were doing.

During a later meeting I kept hearing something about a sum of money. £50 it was.

'You've paid it out for something,' I said to the woman I'd been talking to, but no, she couldn't understand what I meant.

I moved on, but halfway through a message for someone else I had to stop and go back. The £50 wouldn't stop coming until we'd pinned it down.

'I'm sorry,' I said, 'but this £50 is for you and it's something to do with a gas cooker.'

The woman gasped and clapped her hands to her mouth.

'Oh, my God. She's only been over two weeks and I bought her gas cooker. I did pay fifty pounds for it.'

We'd got there. A feeling of satisfaction flooded out from my houseproud contact on the other side.

'She's got a bargain there, too,' said the voice. 'It was nearly brand new.'

'Yes, it was,' agreed the woman. 'Thank her very much.'

Word spread about what was going on and soon other performers would slip into the hall after their own shows and sit quietly on the steps or stand at the back. Little presents started arriving at the theatre for me just as they used to when I was in Australia. One lady gave me a crystal vase just big enough to hold flowers for my spirit children. Someone else brought me a brooch with feathers in it and one old lady gave me some lovely mother-of-pearl shells, all cleaned up and polished. I've put them in my cabinet.

Some people clearly had mixed feelings to start with. I came out of my dressing-room one evening and almost bumped into a woman who was standing determinedly outside the door. She had had no intention of coming she told me. She'd read about my work and thought that if God was going to give anybody a gift like mine he would have given it to priests and nuns not to ordinary housewives.

Yet at the last minute she changed her mind. Something had made her come along to the theatre to see for herself and after the show she was so impressed she felt compelled to come and talk to me. As we chatted I heard a young man's voice in the background. It turned out to be her son who had been killed.

Well, what could I do? I could hardly turn her away so I gave her a quick private sitting. As soon as I tuned in I got a falling feeling as if I'd been thrown and then

I landed on the floor with my fingers across my neck. Apparently it was a car accident and the boy's brother had been driving. Someone called Donald had gone over at the same time.

I wasn't to leave Scotland, however, without stirring up a bit of controversy. It seems to be getting a habit these days, although I don't do it on purpose.

Quite a few reporters came to interview me for the Scottish papers while I was there and during one of these interviews I was asked how I felt about God.

'I mean I don't believe in God,' said the girl turning to a fresh page in her notebook. 'Do you?'

'Oh yes,' I said. 'Without God I couldn't exist and I certainly couldn't do my work.'

The girl frowned. This was obviously not what she wanted to hear.

'Well, how do you stand on the question of Jesus?'

And I told her what I believe. I don't ask anyone else to believe it. I'm not saying it's a hundred per cent right. It just happens to be my view, that's all.

'Well, I think Jesus Christ was the greatest medium and healer who ever lived and that he was put to death for political reasons by the people in the church,' I said. 'They were afraid of him because they realized he had something that the church couldn't offer.'

The girl was scribbling furiously. 'So what about the crucifixion?'

'Well, it happened,' I said, 'but I don't believe that because Jesus was crucified he can wash me free of sin. He can't take responsibility for what I do. Only I can do that. If I do something wrong I can't just walk into church and have the slate wiped clean and go out and do it again. I am responsible for my actions and if I do something wrong I have to pay for it.'

The reporter seemed quite satisfied with this and after

202

a few more questions she packed up her things and left. But when the paper came out, blazed across the column were the words: 'Doris Stokes Doesn't Believe That Jesus Was the Son of God.'

This upset a lot of people and in particular it upset one of my sitters. For three months before the Festival a certain gentleman had been writing to the promoter's office regularly to arrange a private sitting. Then as the Festival drew near he began ringing every few days to check that the booking was still all right. He was assured it was. His appointment was for 12.00, Thursday.

The day of the sitting happened to be the day this newspaper story came out. I was feeling irritable because I'd been misunderstood, but when the doorbell rang at 12.00 I made myself calm down. It wouldn't be fair to take it out on this poor man who had been waiting so long for a sitting.

John went to the door but was surprised to find a young girl standing there.

'I've come to see Doris Stokes,' she said.

'No, I'm sorry there must be some mistake, dear,' he said. 'She's expecting a gentleman any minute now.'

'Oh he's not coming,' said the girl. 'He's given his booking to me.'

Apparently this man had been so angry at what I was supposed to have said in the paper that he refused to come, but since this girl was curious about what I did he said she could go in his place.

John doubtfully let the girl into the hallway and came to talk to me. Rightly or wrongly I was furious when I heard. I thought of all the desperate people in Edinburgh whom we'd had to turn away because all the bookings were taken. All those people who had lost children, or husbands, or wives, and were craving for reassurance. People who would jump at the chance of a cancelled booking, and he thought it would be all right to send someone who was merely curious.

'No,' I said to John, 'I won't do it. I'll save my energy for someone who actually needs help.'

Unhappily John went to relay this message to the girl in the hall. By the time the front door had slammed behind her I was already regretting my harsh words. Maybe I was being unfair. After all, it wasn't the girl's fault. Perhaps I had been too hasty.

Miserably I began leafing through the paper with that unpleasant sensation in my stomach that's caused by a bad conscience. The doorbell rang again. If it's that girl back maybe I should see her I was thinking, when John put his head round the door.

'It's Moira,' he said, 'she's got the date mixed up. You said Friday at 12.00 but she wrote down Thursday at 12.00.'

I sighed with relief. I had done the right thing after all.

I got up and went to the door.

'Never mind, love,' I said. 'You come in.'

I was very glad I was free to see Moira that day. She had travelled a long way to meet me in Edinburgh and she was so heartbroken at the loss of her daughter that she had thought about taking an overdose.

When Morag came to talk to me I felt myself flung violently into the air then there was a pain across my throat. Apparently Morag had been travelling in a car when the door came open and she was thrown out. She hit the pole of a bus stop and was killed instantly. During the sitting she gave the names of her brother and sister and her sister's boyfriend. She also mentioned a photograph that her mother had.

'The jumper I'm wearing in the photo is the one Mum took out of the drawer and held to her face,' she said.

She was very concerned about her mother because of the pills she needed to keep her going in her grief. 'Please don't, Mum,' she kept saying. 'Please don't.'

She was so distressed her mother promised to try to cut down although she didn't feel she could do without them entirely.

Strangely enough while I was in Edinburgh I got the chance to help someone who was normally to be found working only ten minutes away from my home in London.

The producer of the *Jimmy Young Show* had been ringing all round Edinburgh in a desperate attempt to find me. Apparently Jimmy was supposed to be leaving for a publicity tour to publicize his new book but at the last minute he refused to go.

Two incidents had convinced him that he would be in danger. A medium had rung the BBC to say that she had seen a black cloud hovering over Jimmy Young and she thought it was a warning. Then a friend of Jimmy's had gone to a healer and the healer had told him he could see a man connected with him in a plane crash. He saw a small plane and a man slumped inside with a gash on his head.

Jimmy put these two messages together and came to the conclusion that his small plane was going to crash as he travelled the country on the tour. The publishers were desperate. Would I be able to help put his mind at rest?

'Well, I'll talk to him,' I said, 'but if I feel he's in danger I'll have to say so.'

'Well, yes, of course,' they said, 'we don't want anything to happen to him after all. We just wondered if he might be over-reacting.'

I was quite excited as I waited for Jimmy Young to come on the phone. I've always liked his prog, as he calls it, and he has some interesting people appearing.

I was sitting there with the receiver in my hand day-dreaming about whether I should ask him to play a Jim Reeves record for me, when a bright breezy voice suddenly crackled in my ear.

'Hello, Doris? How are you?'

It was Jimmy and sounding exactly like he does on the radio. He explained in more detail about the warnings and how he felt about them.

'Some people might think I'm crazy, Doris,' he said, 'but I don't want to take the risk.'

'Well, just a minute. Let's see if we can find any of your relatives on the other side and ask them,' I said.

I tuned in and after a moment or two I contacted Jimmy's father.

'Tell him not to take any notice,' said the father. 'He'll be all right. I'll be with him and he won't come to any harm.'

I passed on the message along with several other bits and pieces and the result was that Jimmy went on his book tour and afterwards flew on to Australia as well. He sent me an autographed copy of his book as a souvenir.

People still have some strange ideas about our work. When I returned to London I got a letter from a woman who said her vicar had told her she was wicked to read such evil books as mine. I have had quite a few letters like this over the years. The writers are usually upset about the unsympathetic attitude of the clergyman but determined to carry on reading nevertheless.

'I don't care what he says,' they often write, 'nobody else has been able to give me the comfort I've found in your books.'

It's a pity but at the moment the orthodox church can't make up its mind about mediums. Some clergymen regard us as servants of the devil, while others think we're wonderful. On many occasions I've shared the platform with vicars and I even gave the Bishop of Southwark a sitting in Southwark Palace.

Yet funnily enough that incident illustrates the confused attitude of the church to spiritualism. A friend of mine, the Rev Terry Carter, had taken me to meet Mervyn Stockwood who was Bishop at the time. Terry was due to appear on stage with me at our Easter service.

We drove through the enormous gates of Southwark Palace and we were led through beautiful rooms to see the Bishop. I don't know what I expected, but Mervyn Stockwood was certainly no disappointment.

He was sitting on his ornate Bishop's throne in a splendid purple robe and I felt as if I was meeting the King. I was rather nervous to start with but nevertheless we had an interesting sitting and afterwards we fell into general conversation.

Terry Carter had told the Bishop about his plans to conduct the Easter service for us but there was one point on which he needed advice.

'Do you think it would be all right if I wore my collar, Bishop?'

The Bishop thought for a moment or two. 'Oh, I don't think so,' he said doubtfully. 'No, I don't think it would do.'

He wasn't actually forbidding it but his reaction made me cross.

'Well, I think you're a hypocrite,' I burst out before I could stop myself.

The Bishop raised his eyebrows. 'Why do you say that, Doris?' he asked politely.

I'd done it now, I thought, so I might as well have my say. 'Well, look at you,' I said. 'There you sit in all your purple with your Bishop's ring on while I give you a sitting and yet you say Terry shouldn't wear his collar to conduct a religious service. I think that's hypocritical. It ought to be left up to Terry to decide for himself.'

I think he was rather surprised at this outburst but the Bishop was very good about it. He agreed that I had a point and that Terry should let his own conscience guide him on the matter.

And on Good Friday as we prepared ourselves for the meeting at Brixton, the Rev Terry Carter climbed bravely on to the platform wearing his dog collar for all to see.

# CHAPTER 13

The last time I was in hospital an Irish friend came to see me.

'You always seem to be in hospital, Doris,' he said. 'How many operations have you had now?'

Briskly I totted it up on my fingers.

'It must be twelve now,' I said. 'I've had my boob off, my thyroid out, my gall bladder out, my ovaries removed, a hysterectomy and seven other minor operations.'

My friend listened to this impressive list with awe.

'Well, you know what it is, don't you?' he said at last.

'No. What is it?'

'They want you over on the spirit side but they can't have you because you're too busy so they're taking you over piece by piece!'

Well, I just roared with laughter. It was the funniest thing I'd heard in ages. I laughed so much I had to make my friend promise not to crack any more jokes -- it was too much for my stitches.

Yet afterwards it set me thinking. At my age and with all the operations I've had I couldn't help wondering how much time I'd got left. Was this operation going to be my last? I asked Ramanov.

'Ramanov, can you tell me how much time I've got left?'

There was a long silence. Then came one of his typically enigmatic answers.

'You will have enough time to do the work God wants you to do.'

So I wasn't to know. Well, it didn't really matter. I'm not afraid to die. I know it's a great adventure I've got to look forward to and though I'm not in a hurry to leave John and Terry and all the people I love on earth, I'm happy to think that one day I will see my John Michael again. I will be able to take him in my arms and we will never be parted again.

So to all those parents like me who have lost children, I would just like to say, please don't leave your child's room as a shrine. Please don't turn away from those who are left.

Put his toys and clothes to good use. Hug the children who remain, and thank God for the joy of that special child lent to you for a little while, in the sure and certain knowledge that one day when your work is done you will see him again.

Do not stand at my grave and weep . . .
   I am not there – I do not sleep,

I am a thousand winds that blow,
I am the softly falling snow,
I am the gentle rains that fall,
I am the fields of ripening grain.

I am in the morning hush,
I am in the graceful rush
Of beautiful birds in circling flight,
I am the starshine of the night.

I am in the flowers that bloom
I am in a quiet room.
I am in the birds that sing,
I am in each lovely thing.

Do not stand at my grave and cry –
   I did not die . . .

Mary E. Frye
1932

# VOICES IN MY EAR

**Doris Stokes (with Linda Dearsley)**
The Autobiography of a Medium

SHE'S HELPED TO SOLVE MURDER CASES.
SHE FILLED THE SYDNEY OPERA HOUSE THREE
NIGHTS IN A ROW.
ONCE, SHE EVEN HAD TO CONVINCE A MAN HE
WAS DEAD.
NOW SHE'S WRITTEN HER OWN ASTONISHING
LIFE STORY.

Her name is Doris Stokes.

As a child she often saw things others couldn't.
During the War she was officially informed her
husband had been killed. At the height of her grief
she was visited by her long-dead father and told her
husband was alive and would return.

But joy turned to grief when her father reappeared
to warn of the impending death of her healthy baby
son.

Both predictions came true.

And Doris Stokes had to accept the fact that she
possessed an amazing gift. Exceptional psychic
powers that over the years of her extraordinary life
have brought joy and comfort to thousands of
people.

FUTURA PUBLICATIONS
NON-FICTION/AUTOBIOGRAPHY
0 7088 1786 6

## MORE VOICES IN MY EAR

**Doris Stokes (with Linda Dearsley)**
Sequel to the bestselling *VOICES IN MY EAR*

SINCE THE PUBLICATION OF HER ASTONISHING
LIFE STORY, THE BESTSELLING *VOICES IN MY
EAR*, MEDIUM DORIS STOKES HAS BEEN
BESIEGED BY REQUESTS FROM HER MANY NEW
FRIENDS TO RECOUNT MORE OF HER UNIQUE
EXPERIENCES.

Now in MORE VOICES IN MY EAR she tells how her
extraordinary psychic powers have helped the
family of one of the Yorkshire Ripper victims,
enabled the late actor Peter Finch to communicate
with his wife, and brought hope to the parents of
young children who have disappeared in strange
circumstances all over the world.

Writing of her experiences in Australia and New
Zealand, America and Canada and in Ireland, Doris
now gives a complete picture of life in the spirit
world and never fails to comfort and encourage all
her many friends and followers.

FUTURA PUBLICATIONS
NON-FICTION
0 7088 2100 6

All Futura Books are available at your bookshop or newsagent, or can be ordered from the following address:
Futura Books, Cash Sales Department,
P.O. Box 11, Falmouth, Cornwall TR10 9EN.

Please send cheque or postal order (no currency), and allow 60p for postage and packing for the first book plus 25p for the second book and 15p for each additional book ordered up to a maximum charge of £1.90 in U.K.

B.F.P.O. customers please allow 60p for the first book, 25p for the second book plus 15p per copy for the next 7 books, thereafter 9p per book.

Overseas customers, including Eire, please allow £1.25 for postage and packing for the first book, 75p for the second book and 28p for each subsequent title ordered.